P9-BJB-604

# persuasion

>> command attention
>> hold their interest
>> get what you want

Tom Gorman

BUSINESS

Adams Media

Avon, Massachusetts

Copyright © 2007 by F+W Publications. All rights reserved.
This book, or parts thereof, may not be reproduced in any form without
permission from the publisher; exceptions are made for brief excerpts used
in published reviews.

Published by Adams Business, an imprint of Adams Media,
an F+W Publications Company
57 Littlefield Street
Avon, MA 02322
www.adamsmedia.com

ISBN 10: 1-59869-100-7
ISBN 13: 978-1-59869-100-9

Printed in Canada.

J I H G F E D C B A

Library of Congress Cataloging-in-Publication Data
is available from the publisher.

This publication is designed to provide accurate and authoritative information with regard to the subject matter covered. It is sold with the understanding that the publisher is not engaged in rendering legal, accounting,
or other professional advice. If legal advice or other expert assistance is
required, the services of a competent professional person should be sought.
—From a *Declaration of Principles* jointly adopted by a Committee of the
American Bar Association and a Committee of Publishers and Associations

Many of the designations used by manufacturers and sellers to distinguish
their product are claimed as trademarks. Where those designations appear
in this book and Adams Media was aware of a trademark claim, the designations have been printed with initial capital letters.

*This book is available at quantity discounts for bulk purchases.*
*For information, please call 1-800-289-0963.*

# contents

part
3

## PERSUASION PARTICULARS

# introduction

# Read this book, and you'll be rich!

Okay, I'll be rich too. But that's the way the world works. To get what you want, you've got to give people what they want. To get attention, you've got to appeal to a basic need, and that's what I'm doing. We both want to be rich, right? Watch, and learn.

To persuade anyone to do anything—even to listen to you— you've got to show them, clearly and quickly, what's in it for them. Most of the time. Sometimes you need to tease and intrigue them and appeal to their curiosity or sense of humor. Hey, persuasion isn't easy, which is why you need this book.

In this book you'll learn an essential business and life skill. You'll learn how to persuade people to give you their attention, to consider your point of view, and to support your efforts to succeed.

How will you do this? By seeing what persuasion really is, why and how it works, and what you must do to practice the art of persuasion. Wait, didn't I just say it was a skill? It is a skill and an art—plus science. It's psychology, sociology, economics, and communication, but not the way they're taught in school. Persuasion puts all those things together at the person-to-person, in-the-moment action level. Success at persuasion depends on knowing what makes people tick, then showing them that the time has come to go along with you.

Wherever you're going and whatever you're doing, you're going to need other people's help. But this raises questions, especially if you're in the early years of your working life: Who are these people?

Where do I find them? How do I talk to them? Why should they listen to me? What do I have to offer them?

You'll find the answers to those questions—and more—in this easy-reading volume.

## What Is Persuasion?

For our purposes, persuasion is inducing one or more people to willingly and knowingly do something for you that they hadn't initially planned or even wanted to do. Usually, they will resist you and have more power than you, which is why you need persuasion. Persuasion is getting people interested in doing as you suggest when they're originally not particularly interested in that.

Persuasion works by influencing the other person to change. They are going to do something that they didn't initially want to do, and they are going to do it because of you. You, as the persuader, are an agent of change.

## Everybody Does It

Everybody uses persuasion, and uses it often. You're going to see persuasion whenever someone can grant or withhold something that someone else wants or needs. Persuasion applies in a huge range of professional and personal situations, including these:

- *You need more time, money, or other resources from your boss*

- *You're selling a product or service.*

- *You have to raise money for a project or business.*

- *You want to break into a highly competitive field.*

- *You want admission to a certain type of school to learn a new vocation or avocation.*

- *You need to get past gatekeepers and gain access to people you want to persuade.*

- *You need to resolve a problem with a service provider.*

- *You simply want to get your way more often.*

I myself have used persuasion to get a literary agent, win book contracts, sell products and services, gain promotions to better positions, and get approval for increased budgets, new hires, extended deadlines, and special projects. I have been a midlevel manager in Fortune 500 companies, an executive recruiter, a workshop facilitator, a salesman, a product manager, a new product developer, and, for the past ten years, a freelance writer.

The common thread in situations that call of persuasion is the need to influence people. This requires leading people or pushing them, chasing them or playing hard to get, pressuring them or leaving them alone. It all depends on the situation and the people involved, including you. The more you know about persuasion and the more tools you have at your disposal, the more effective you will be.

Whatever you want to become and whatever you want to accomplish, there are people who can help you. But you have to ask them to help you—usually more than once—give them good reasons to help you, and make them feel good about helping you. That's persuasion, and you can learn how to do it.

Can I persuade you to turn to Chapter 1, so you can start learning how?

> **NOT BRUTE FORCE** BUT ONLY PERSUASION AND FAITH ARE THE KINGS OF THIS WORLD.
>
> —Thomas Carlyle
> (British historian)

# Learn to Persuade, and You'll Always Succeed

1

When you hear the word persuasion, what do you picture in your mind? Maybe you see a slick Hollywood agent working the phones, or a politician working the podium. Maybe you think of a Mafia don making offers people can't refuse. Or a flim-flam man conning people out of fortunes.

> ## per•suas•ion
> 1. Inducing someone to do something they initially resisted
> 2. Influencing someone more powerful than you to do as you ask

The people in those stereo-typical images often do persuade, with fast talk, trickery, begging, power plays, and pressure. These can be tools of persuasion, but for most of us they're not the most effective ones—at least not when used that blatantly.

Some researchers claim that all communication involves persuasion at some level but we here we're talking about specific tools for influencing others. The tools of persuasion that I'll cover include flatter-

1

ing, reasoning, amusing, arguing, agreeing, insisting, badgering, soliciting, lobbying, challenging, bragging, threatening (in ethical ways), empathizing, apologizing, seducing, scorekeeping, bargaining, trading, storytelling, piggybacking, and persisting.

It's quite an arsenal, but they all fit within a larger method. That larger method enables you to prepare a plan, locate and gain access to the people you need to persuade, engage their attention, present your case, deal with resistance, and secure their agreement.

## Focus versus Hocus-pocus

I should mention that I stick to what works, and I'm not keen on methods that I don't find persuasive. Some authors and Web-site operators claim that they'll teach you to secretly hypnotize people, establish magical rapport, lower their resistance, and get them to do things like drive you to the airport. I realize that most communication occurs on subconscious levels, which is where the methods I've just mentioned supposedly operate, but I've never met anyone who found them useful, and I still have to take taxis to the airport.

However, those methods aren't totally useless. If nothing else, they may help

**Take Action**
Browse www.workingpsychology.com/marwell.html for Marwell & Schmitt's taxonomy of sixteen influence tactics.

you to focus on the other person, develop (or at least exhibit) an interest them, and maybe gain insight into their motives and emotions. Any of those outcomes would be useful, yet I suspect that researching their professional and personal backgrounds and listening closely to them would work better than trying to hypnotize them.

## But Isn't Persuasion Manipulation?

Sort of. In persuasion, you attempt to influence other people's beliefs or behavior to achieve your purposes. Your purposes may be as lofty as Martin Luther King's or as low as a snake oil salesman's. But manipulation depends on whether the person being persuaded (whom I call the receiver or persuadee) feels manipulated, and whether the persuader is sincere.

## ARENAS OF PERSUASION

- Advertising, selling, and public relations

- Politicking and speechmaking

- Networking and job seeking

- Dealing with everyday human relations

## The Ethics of Persuasion

Professional persuaders, such as lawyers and advertisers, can usually argue either side of an issue. They can even do this while seeming completely sincere, which hasn't helped sincerity's standing. But that underscores the fact that persuasion is a skill, like swimming or cooking—but with a difference. With persuasion, you are influencing people to do something they might not have done without your influence. Therefore, you have some moral obligation to the people you persuade.

The chief responsibility is to be honest. Some professional persuaders will say, "Well, they're big boys and girls who can make their own decisions." Real persuasion is convincing people to *willingly* and *knowingly* do as you ask. They can't do that if you've deceived them. You must act ethically.

**eth•ics**

1. Guidelines for behavior that are rooted in judgments about right and wrong
2. Code of proper or allowable behavior for a profession or organization

## The Goal: Change Beliefs and Behavior

The goal of persuasion is to change someone's beliefs and behavior. You might think that changing behavior would be enough, but beliefs dictate our behavior. Unless someone believes you can do a job, they won't hire you to do it. So you must get them to believe you can do the job so they will exhibit the desired behavior and hire you.

Think of persuasion as the process of moving someone from Point A, their original point of view, to Point B, your point of view. Or if it's a long way from their point of view to yours, move them from Point A to Point B to Point C, and so on. In other words, if you understand your receivers' thoughts and feelings on a subject, then you can chart a path to your viewpoint or to interim points that will lead to your viewpoint.

## Appealing to the Head and the Heart

What is more effective: appealing to reason or emotion? Well, it depends on whom you're trying to persuade, and what you're trying to persuade them to do. It depends on how they view the situation and how they process information, and on the stage of the persuasion process.

To cover your bases, try to appeal to the head *and* the heart. Companies selling investments emphasize the financial return, but also use emotional appeals featuring silver-haired couples frolicking on golf courses, and college graduates in mortarboards. Similarly, charities portray the suffering of the afflicted, but also mention that the money goes to help the people who need it, rather than to pay administrative expenses. The companies and charities just mentioned do these things because people make decisions using both reason and emotion. They have to *think* something is a good idea and *feel* it's a good idea. Also, most people lean more toward thinking or toward feeling their way to a decision, so it's wise to strike a balance in your messages, at least until you learn how your receiver makes decisions.

In business, it's easy to believe that the rational appeal is always most effective. But even there you often have to appeal to a person's ego, competitiveness, sense of humor, or fear of looking bad. Few decisions are devoid of emotion. Even in sales of business-to-business products, such as photocopiers or industrial adhesives, skilled salespeople help customers feel that they'll look good to their bosses, triumph over competitors, or enter the ranks of the forward thinking by buying the product.

## KEY STEPS

○ Persuade yourself

○ Research and plan

○ Engage and pitch

○ Navigate and negotiate

## Four Steps to Persuasion

As with any skill, there are proven ways to go about persuading people to do things:

### Number 1: Persuade Yourself

You'll have a hard time persuading someone to back your proposal if you lack confidence in it. Conversely, if you are confident in it, you stand an excellent chance of persuading others to come on board. Belief is contagious, and so is disbelief.

As someone who spent too long in too many jobs that I didn't enjoy, I can tell you this: when you believe in what you're doing, you will see far more success than when you don't.

## Number 2: Research Your Receiver and Plan Your Approach

Research helps you identify who to approach and what to discuss. It enables you to identify and create potential wins for people, and to say smart things and ask smart questions when you approach them. It also helps you to anticipate and address potential points of resistance. All of this builds your confidence so you can be more persuasive.

## Number 3: Engage Your Receiver and Make Your Pitch

After you get your receiver on the phone or enter his office, you must soon present your proposal or plan. By proposal or plan, I mean anything from asking for time, information or contacts; to requesting their participation in a project or investment; to proposing that you work for them as an employee, consultant, or supplier.

This is the point where you usually—but not always—must answer the question that the receiver will pose in some form: "What's in it for me?" I say "not always" because many people will give you their time or share information or contacts and expect nothing but gratitude. But they still must be persuaded that you won't waste their time, misuse their information, or embarrass them in front of their contacts. As marketing consultant Todd Domke points out, "People can be very generous about opening up their networks of friends and associates to you, as long as they like you and trust you. If they don't like you and trust you, the trail ends with them." Getting people to like and trust you basically comes down to being informed, professional, respectful, and appreciative.

## The Power of Research

In *What Color Is Your Parachute?* Richard Nelson Bolles suggests that job seekers deeply research organizations they're interested in working for, first in written and online sources and then by interviewing for information with people in the organizations. The process often leads to actual job interviews and can even help you to persuade an employer to create a job for you. It's still one of the most effective job-search tactics around.

When you want more than time, information, or contacts, be prepared to provide examples of financial, professional, and strategic wins that benefit the person or her organization—as well as emotional wins. Be prepared to meet objections and to discuss the receiver's needs frankly. Be ready to handle unexpected news and setbacks on the way to your goal. Be armed with emotional appeals in case you need them. In other words, be totally prepared to make your pitch and support your proposal.

## Number 4:
## Navigate Roadblocks
## and Negotiate Agreement

To persuade someone to a course of action, you must deal with differences in viewpoint, objections to your proposal, and refusals to take the next step. Often it's best to deal with differences indirectly to avoid challenging the receiver. Sometimes, however, it's better to challenge them.

In other words, dealing with differences is something of an art. First, to deal directly with a difference you must get the person to state a specific objection. Some people will tell you quite frankly what they don't like about your idea. Others will tell you they like it, yet refuse to take the next step. They'll say things like, "It's not right for us right now," or "Everybody loved it, but it doesn't fit our current strategy." It's hard to deal with these objections because they're not specific. So the first step is to learn what, specifically, keeps someone from moving toward your point of view.

Then the real work begins: developing and delivering the logical or emotional appeals that will defuse, overcome, or minimize the objections. For instance, if someone says that what you're proposing costs too much or takes too long or involves too many people, you can try to persuade them that the result is worth the cost, time, or manpower it will require. Or you can reduce their cost, time, or manpower commitment. Or you can point out that the cost, time, or manpower amounts to very little compared with that necessary for less-worthy endeavors. Or you can offer guarantees.

When someone is persuaded—that is, when they've logically embraced, or at least accepted, your point of view and feel positively toward your proposal—obtaining final agreement is usually straightforward. Yet many people often need a push to make the final commitment and actually give you the name of their contact, a big check, or a formal agreement. So always ask them to take the final step, and to agree to a specific timeframe or deadline.

## Think Win-Win—No, Really

You've probably heard about thinking win-win and building win-win relationships. However, since we are all mainly concerned with ourselves, it might sound like a line to you. Yet win-win is the only way to work effectively with people. You have to look out for yourself and the other guy. You have to actively seek wins for anyone you want to persuade. If you can't find wins for them, you must try to create wins for them, even if it is only discussing the potential effect your proposal may have.

> Unless both sides win, no agreement can be permanent.
> —Jimmy Carter
> (U.S. President)

So think win-win and seek and create wins for them. These wins can range from magnificent financial rewards to the simple joy of helping someone get ahead. Without mentioning these wins, however, you'll find it hard to be persuasive.

## Persuasive Persistence

In my experience, the two most important success factors in persuasion are locating people who are willing and able to help you, and then not giving up. Marketers, those paragons of persuasion, must accomplish these goals, and one way they do this is by showing persistence. Today, they expend more resources than ever on locating and cultivating customers, and, God knows, they never give up.

Persistence will boost your persuasiveness in several ways:

**Take Action**

*For information on creating wins, get hold of* Business Is a Contact Sport *by Tom Richardson and Augusto Vidaurreta with Tom Gorman. It's out of print but still available.*

- If you look long enough, you will eventually find people who will be receptive to your plan or proposal.

- If you try to persuade enough people, your skills improve as you learn how to discover their motives, read their responses, and adjust your approaches.

- If you persist—in the right way—with specific people, either you will wear them down or you will become familiar to them and thus become a known quantity.

All three of these benefits of persistence are important, but many people fail to consider that last one. The first book I wrote was with Paul Miller, an executive-development consultant. I met Paul at a church we both attended, and when I learned about his work, I pitched him the idea of doing a business book together. When I first broached the idea to him, he politely turned me down. He would do the same a few times over the next two years. Then, however, we worked together on a committee and he realized that I was reasonably sensible, professional, and trustworthy. The next time I approached him, he agreed to share his materials with me so we could explore the idea of writing a book.

Was this persuasion? Definitely. After Paul got to know me, he was willing to explore the possibility of a book project.

Mind you, I still had to show that I understood his material and the kind of book he wanted to write. I still had to write a book proposal that would persuade an agent to take on the project, and persuade a publisher to give us a book contract.

It all worked out. I wrote the book proposal, which got me an agent who sold it to a publisher. Then I collaborated with Paul on the book (*Big League Business Thinking*), which became the first of many I would write.

## You Can Be Very Persuasive

You may be a seasoned attorney, salesperson, or negotiator just looking for a few new ideas on persuasion. Or you might be a recent college grad trying to persuade someone to give you a chance to show your stuff in a competitive line of work. In any case, the question is: Can you become more persuasive?

The answer is yes, because persuasion really is as much a skill as it is an art.

### Columbus Persisted

Queen Isabella of Spain rejected Columbus's petition to finance his voyage twice, but he won on his third try. What worked? He appealed to her need for gold, desire to conquer Japan, and intention of spreading Catholicism. Instead, the voyage brought Spain to the Americas and into an age of global power.

" THE **REAL PERSUADERS** ARE OUR APPETITES, OUR FEARS AND ABOVE ALL OUR VANITY. "

—Eric Hoffer
(author)

# Changing the Balance of Power

2

You need persuasion when you can't get what you want simply by asking. By their nature, requests can be denied. In this chapter we're going to look at the balance of power in situations in which you need to use persuasion, and at ways of shifting that balance. We'll also examine the tools at your disposal, and at persuaders as agents of change.

## Why We Need Persuasion

As noted in Chapter 1, we need persuasion when the balance of power works against us in a situation. Recognizing the need for persuasion begins with understanding that the other party has the option of refusing you. They have more power in the situation, but you are not powerless.

First, you have power in virtually any ongoing personal relationship. If you ask

## PEOPLE WITH LESS POWER

- Job seekers

- Professionals with hardnosed clients

- Salespeople

- Those who propose

### h•ier•arch•y

1. Organization in which people have various positions with various ranks
2. Situation in which people of higher rank have power over people of lower rank

your friend, partner, or spouse for something and they refuse, they know, or at least suspect, that you'll make a mental note of that. Then the next time they ask you for something, you might refuse because they refused your request. Also, the next time you ask for that thing or for something else, you may have more leverage because of that refusal.

However, I want to focus on situations in which you have less power than you would in an ongoing personal relationship. These are situations where you have less power because you are lower in a hierarchy or you lack a relationship with the person who can help you. In almost any situation, the person who wants something is, by definition, less powerful than the person who can supply or withhold that thing.

Here are examples of what I mean:

- You are a job applicant. You want an interview, a job offer, and certain conditions of employment—all things that the hiring authority can refuse.

- You are a professional who wants to guide a client, who, in turn, can refuse to listen to you or even fire you.

- *You are a salesperson trying to get an appointment or close a deal, and the customer can evade, avoid, or refuse you.*

## Persuasion Works the Balance of Power

Persuasion doesn't necessarily change the balance of power, although it can. Usually, it shifts the balance of power toward you in some respect, or it works the balance of power in your favor. For example, the balance of power shifts toward the seller when the customer decides that he wants what's being sold. The balance of power has worked in the pleading convict's favor when a judge grants a request for clemency.

> ### bal•ance of pow•er
> 1. Relative influence that parties in a relationship have over one another
> 2. Relationship characterized by competing wants and needs

But another dynamic is often at work in efforts to tilt the balance of power. I and many other parents have been badgered into buying a dog for a child who wouldn't let up, but with motives other than ending the badgering. In my case, I bought the dog because my son finally convinced me that he really, truly, deeply wanted the dog—and a particular puppy at that, which would not be at the pet store forever.

After a certain point, someone with the power to give something to someone will often do it because they are touched by the persuader's sincerity or just want to make him happy. Also, my son, who was only eight years old at the time, persuaded me to see the specific puppy he wanted at the pet store (which I made the mistake of doing). Specifics make a case far more persuasive than a vague desire for "a dog" or "a job" or "a spouse." How persuasive would you find a job applicant who just wanted a job, or a prospective spouse who just wanted to be married?

## Who's Got the Power?

Usually the persuadee has something you want or need, and you have less to offer them, or they have a large set of choices and you are just one of the many they can choose, or they stand above you in a hierarchical relationship. Here are examples of each of these situations:

- *They have something you want, and you have less to offer: you want to buy a particular house or a car but you can't meet the asking price.*

- *They have many choices, of which, you're one: you are applying for a job, competing for a spot, or auditioning for a part that at least several other people want.*

- *They stand above you in a hierarchy: you want to transfer to another area of your organization, or you want to work on a special project, and your boss may not like the idea of losing you or your taking on that work.*

Persuasive techniques shift the balance of power in your favor, even when that balance weighs heavily against you.

> Every man has enough power left to carry out that of which he is convinced.
> —**Johann Wolfgang Von Goethe (German poet)**

## David, Find Your Slingshot

When you are pitching a project to a huge company or applying for a job at one that can choose from hundreds of candidates, it may seem as if the balance of power is hopelessly against you. Yet in the biblical story of David and Goliath, David brought down a giant by hitting him between the eyes with a single stone from his slingshot.

What do you have that will enable you to approach these people with David's confidence and skill?

- *The Goliaths who are the hiring authorities at large organizations need competent people who they can get along with, so if you're competent and likable, you've got an advantage over the merely competent.*

- *The Goliaths of the movie and publishing industries cannot exist without the material provided by creative Davids.*

○ The traffic cop who pulled you over, or the judge you are appearing before is in his position because he enjoys having power; in their uniforms or behind their benches, they are Goliaths, but they also enjoy using their power to give a David a break now and then.

○ The companies that you are trying to sell something to buy products and services every day; in fact, most of the money that these Goliaths don't spend on salaries goes to purchasing products and services, and what you are selling is at least as useful as what they're already purchasing from the other Davids of the world.

## Tipping the Balance of Power

To change the balance of power, you analyze the situation and use the technique that you believe will work best. This is where the *art* of persuasion comes into play. You must scope things out and choose the approach that will suit that person in that situation, several of which I present here:

### Make yourself stand out:

In any situation in which you are one of many choices, try to stand out in positive ways. Use humor, make a personal connection, take an interest in the other person, or perhaps wear something memorable but tasteful. An interesting approach or pastime, like, say, showing up on a motorcycle, can make you memorable for the right reasons when it suits the situation.

**Increase the value or perceived value of your offer:** In negotiating situations, which we'll discuss in depth in Chapter 7, and when seeking a job, which I cover in Chapter 9, if you can increase your value—or how others perceive your value—relative to your competitors, you may tip the balance your way. For instance, if you're willing (and able) to bring an extra skill or two to the table, or you won't need some type of training, or you speak a second language, play that up. In certain situations, charging less than your competitors can put more money in your persuadee's pocket, thus increasing your value to them. But sometimes charging *more* than competitors can add to the perception of value—provided you deliver commensurate quality.

**Enhance their status:** In certain situations, you may be able to somehow enhance the persuadee's position or status. When possible, try to make them appear as important to the endeavor as they are—or even more important. For instance, offer them a chance for publicity, a by-lined article, or an introduction to a celebrity, if they take part in the project.

**Lower their risk:** Often, the process of persuasion is the process of helping someone cope with risk. If you can offer a guarantee, such as working until they're satisfied, capping their exposure, or redoing the job for free if the results don't last, you've made yourself much more attractive.

**Make it easy for them to do what you ask:** Offer to do the research or legwork that the other person would have to do to comply with your request. Or offer to pay for any out-of-pocket expenses they would incur, make all the necessary arrangements, throw a fabulous lunch in with the deal, anything that makes your offer attractive, effortless, and cost free.

**Acknowledge power:** Sometimes simply saying, "Look, I could really use your help. I know there's nothing in it for you besides the satisfaction of helping a fellow human being, but it would mean a lot to me." Okay, it's not far removed from pleading or begging, but it can be very effective.

## What Do People Want?

In situations in which you are trying to persuade someone, you must be aware that people want certain things. One of those things people want is to be left alone to do what they were doing before you came along. That works against you. However, people also want other things that work in your favor:

- *People want respect and recognition.*

- *People want fairness, caring, and support.*

- *People want to work with engaging people.*

- *People want novelty . . .*

**Take Action**
*If you haven't read the classic business book* How to Win Friends and Influence People *by Dale Carnegie, do so. If you have read it, do so again.*

## The Change Process

If persuasion is changing someone's beliefs and behavior, then you'd best know a bit about the change process. This process applies both to significant changes, which require major alterations of beliefs and behaviors, and to small ones.

In a typical change process, a person goes through five stages in which they:

**1.** Become aware that they may need to change

**2.** Acknowledge that they probably should change

**3.** Understand the nature of the change and their alternatives

**4.** Commit to making the change and then take action

**5.** Stick with the change

## Pull, Don't Push

One common mistake is pushing someone to take a step before they're ready. Many salespeople do this, and it heightens resistance. Persuasion is a process of building trust, explaining your proposal, answering questions, and moving to the next level of commitment. For instance, people want to know they won't waste their time by meeting with you, so invest the time and effort to persuade them that they won't be by giving them some solid information and mentioning potential benefits of meeting you, rather than using only teasers, beforehand.

Your job, as persuader, is to assist people in taking each of those steps. Let's look at the dynamic between the persuader and persuadee at each stage of the change process.

### Become Aware That They Need To Change

If the persuadee doesn't know he needs to change, you (the persuader) can generate awareness by bringing up the subject, problem, or whatever it is that you want to persuade them to do. There are hundreds of ways of doing this. Some are direct, as in, "I'm calling to learn whether your agency uses freelance writers." Some are indirect, as in, "Do you want to improve your professional image?"

### Key to Success

It's important to get the attention of the persuadee in a positive way. Often, the challenge is to stand out from the competition. In most cases of person-to-person persuasion, you will do best by learning beforehand about the situation, background, and needs of the persuadee. We'll look at ways of doing this in Chapter 4.

> The best way to persuade people is with your ears—by listening to them.
> —**Dean Rusk**
> **(American diplomat)**

## Acknowledge That They Probably Should Change

To help persuadees acknowledge that they should probably change, you start talking about the benefits of making the change and how you or your organization could help them realize those benefits. It's also very useful to mention how others have made the change and how well you method has worked for them. It's also where you get a conversation going and start building trust by getting him to talk about their current situation, their goals, and the gap between the two. At this point, you help the persuadee see that what you are asking is relevant to him, and that there's some kind of win in it for him.

### Keys to Success

The persuadee has to see what you're proposing as relevant to him. This means doing your homework so you'll approach the right person in the right way. It also means listening, that is, active listening, not the kind of listening where you're just waiting to say what you want to say.

In active listening you attend closely to what the speaker is saying with the goal of understanding not only what they are saying, but also the mindset and emotions behind what they are saying. You also encourage the speaker to talk and you refrain from judging him or her. This is part of using the reflective technique which I'll discuss in Chapter 7.

**act•ive lis•ten•ing**

1. Listening without interrupting, but with occasional questions to clarify things and comments offering encouragement and empathy
2. Understanding what a person is feeling, as well as saying

## Understand the Nature of the Change and Their Alternatives

Here's where the persuadee asks, "What, exactly, do you want me to do?" That question, or one like it, signals that the process is moving forward, but it's by no means over. The persuadee is really asking, "How much effort, energy, time, or money must I expend?" It will also occur to them that there are alternatives, such as buying a competitor's product, hiring someone else, or ending the entire interaction right then and there. You want to make your proposal the most attractive alternative.

*Without trust, there is nothing.*
**—Anonymous**

### *Keys to Success*

Make it as easy as possible for them to do as you ask, but do not mislead them about what's involved.

One way is to present the next step in the process and see how they feel about that. For example, the next step in your sales process might be to assess their current accounting system or to gather financial information from them. If they then ask about the step after that, then you are continuing the conversation, and that's progress. Yet they may wonder about risks and about whether they can trust you, so take steps to limit their risk and to continue to build trust. For instance, explain that when you assess their system, it's done by professionals who will not disturb your operation, or that when you gather financial information, you keep it strictly confidential.

## Commit to Making the Change and Then Taking Action

Here's where you close the deal, but it doesn't have to be the whole deal. It can be the next step. If you've planned properly, you'll know exactly what the next step is.

### Keys to Success

Make sure the persuadee is comfortable with what you've proposed. If you sense they are not, say, "Are you comfortable with everything I've said so far?" If you don't get a firm, positive response, say, "What aspect of what I'm proposing gives you pause?" However, at the right moment you have to ask for a commitment, even it it's only to take a small step.

## Sticking with the Change

You want people to feel good that they did what you persuaded them to do, rather than second-guessing. Post-persuasion remorse occurs when you push, rather than lead, someone to a decision.

### Key to Success

Express caring and continued interest after you persuade the person. Send an e-mail thanking them, and reinforce the fact that they made the right decision.

## Avenues of Influence

Becoming a skilled persuader means using various forms of influence. The most important ones are the following:

**Trust:** This is the essential condition, and I'll cover it in Chapter 6. When people trust you, they believe what you say.

**Expertise:** People trust experts as individuals who know more than they do in their sphere of expertise. But bad advice or lack of professionalism can undermine your expertise.

**Third-party support:** Endorsements in any form are among the most useful tools of persuasion.

**Fear:** When people fear something, they can be prompted to take steps to avoid that outcome. For that reason, fear should be used judiciously and ethically.

**Punishment:** Withdrawing something, such as your attention, presence, or services is the kind of punishment I mean. In other words, playing hard to get can be a form of punishment.

**Pressure:** There are various forms of pressure you can use to prompt people to act. Two of the most common are limited-time offers and once-in-a-lifetime opportunities.

**Appeals to conscience:** Asking people to "do the right thing" casts the decision to do as you say as a moral choice. Certain persuaders can position the decision to buy their product, for example life insurance or a security system, as a moral choice.

Persuasion influences the balance of power by using specific tools. Learning what those tools are and how and when to use them is essential to persuasion.

" WITH ANY PART YOU PLAY, THERE IS A
CERTAIN AMOUNT OF YOURSELF IN IT.
THERE HAS TO BE, OTHERWISE
IT'S JUST NOT ACTING.
IT'S LYING. "

—Johnny Depp
(actor)

# First Persuade Yourself

In business, as in most areas of life, we are are playing roles, but in the sense that we all play roles as part of our identities. These include roles we play for one another in families, such as father, mother, and son, as well as professional roles, such as teacher, journalist, doctor, manager, and customer. In these various roles we act in the way associated with the role.

In other words, although each of us is always the same person, we behave differently toward the people in our lives, depending on our role relationship with them. Now, what about the role of persuader?

## Listen Closely

When asked about the most important part of acting, most actors say "listening." By listening, they free themselves to respond with the facial and physical gestures that make sense for those characters in that scene.

## Inside Out Persuasion

Most of us have called in sick to work when we weren't really ill or have excused ourselves from a social event by saying we had to work that evening when that really wasn't the case. In these circumstances, many of us have also found that we actually start feeling a little ill or start believing that we really have to get some work done right away.

If you are out to persuade someone to do something, it's best that you believe it yourself. You should believe what you are saying. The surest way for that to happen is to utter only absolutely true statements, or, within the bounds of ethics, to convince yourself that you believe that what you are saying is true.

For example, consider salespeople, executives, and politicians. A salesperson selling Acme vacuum cleaners tells his customers that they are the best on the market—until he's hired by the SuperVac company, at which point he changes his story. The politician opposes gun control, until his constituents support it.

You can say, "Well, yeah, but they're being paid to represent a certain product or group of people," and that's true. But they all changed their thinking and their expressed positions, and became ready to persuade others to that new way of thinking. Were they lying before they changed their positions? Probably not. Instead, they were reducing their cognitive dissonance by convincing themselves they believed that what they were saying was true.

In fact, when you find yourself feeling queasy after you call in sick or you actually wind up working on the night of the social event, you are reducing your cognitive dissonance. After all, you're an honest person, right? So you are feeling a little bit ill, aren't you? And you did wind up working that night, didn't you?

## Getting Your Head Straight

Cognitive dissonance occurs in our minds when related thoughts, beliefs, intentions, or actions are out of sync. One common example occurs in divorces and break-ups. The partner who wants out starts seeing only the negative aspects of the other partner. Things that once seemed attractive, such as a military sense of order or a cute laugh, now seem irritating.

Why? Because when we do something or make a decision, it has to make sense to us, and we build a case in our minds so that it does make sense to us. You wouldn't break up with a terrific

### cog•nit•ive diss•o•nance

1. Psychological discomfort caused by thinking one way and acting another, for instance not wearing seat belts when you know they save lives 2. Feelings that people reduce by rationalization or behavior change, for instance by saying they would rather be thrown clear of the wreckage or by starting to wear seat belts

partner, would you? Well, then you have to persuade yourself that they are not terrific after all.

What does this have to do with persuasion?

To practice persuasion you must first persuade yourself, and then persuade your receiver, of the soundness of your proposal, plan, or proposition. You can't pick up the phone or go into a meeting not believing what you are about to persuade someone about. That would create cognitive dissonance in your mind. As a result, you will communicate your conflicted belief to your receiver, even if you think your won't. You have to persuade yourself before you can persuade them. Let's look at some legitimate ways you can use to persuade yourself.

***Take Action***
*Visit* www.apa.org/books/4318830s.html *and read* An Introduction to Cognitive Dissonance Theory and an Overview of Current Perspectives on the Theory. *It's a bit technical, but clear and informative.*

## Reducing Real Dissonance

Cognition has to do with perception, and reducing cognitive dissonance is largely a mental exercise. I have no problem with mental exercises, but I find it easier to persuade myself of something if I take actions that change my perceptions. Then I have real reasons to be persuaded.

For instance, thinking I'm a great public speaker is all well and good. I could even look in the mirror every morning and say, "I am an excellent public speaker. People enjoy listening to what I say, and I enjoy saying it." But if I haven't prepared myself in other ways, I know I'm going to be toast when I get in front of an audience.

So before any public-speaking engagement, I learn whatever I can about the audience, why they're in front of me, and what they expect to learn. I try to relate my material to their concerns, structure a solid presentation, and anticipate their questions. I make sure the room and my audiovisual materials are squared away beforehand. Only then am I persuaded that I am going to give them a first-rate presentation, and only then can I persuade them with confidence. (I'll cover persuasive speeches and presentations in Chapter 11.)

> "Let one who wants to move and convince others, first be convinced and moved themselves.
> —**Thomas Carlyle**

Planning and preparation will carry you to success. You have to prepare yourself mentally and emotionally, and prepare a solid proposal, research your persuadee, know what you want to say, and anticipate responses. In doing all this preparation, you will usually persuade yourself that you have a valid proposition and the ability to present it well. In other words, mental and emotional preparation comes down to developing confidence in your proposal and in your ability to present it.

## The Confidence Game

The expression "con," as in fraud, is short for confidence. Thus a con game is a confidence game, and a con artist is a confidence artist. The term "confidence" here means taking someone into your confidence. Typically, the con man is willing to let someone in on a terrific deal on a confidential basis, which is supposedly why the victim isn't supposed to tell anyone else (who may be less gullible or greedy) about the deal. Of course, the con artist needs a lot of confidence to pull this off.

Now I am not suggesting that you con anyone. I am, however, suggesting that you develop a bit of the con artist's confidence. After all, if a con artist can exude all that confidence when he's ripping someone off, you can certainly do the same when you are persuading someone to support your completely legitimate plan or proposal.

Now, how do cons do it? They play to the victim's greed on the one hand, and naiveté on the other. They usually let the victim feel that he's in control and give him ample opportunity to back out of the deal—after they have made it utterly irresistible. And they make it appear as if the victim is in a no-risk situation, usually by putting in some of what appears to be their own money. They also dress and act the part, complete with the appropriate props,

### Take Action
*Buy or rent the DVD of the Stephen Spielberg film* Catch Me If You Can, *starring Leo DiCaprio as master con man Frank Abagnale, Jr. Among other things, it's a fascinating study of people's willingness to take others at face value.*

and do so with utter confidence. Above all, they win the victim's trust.

Although con artists are despicable criminals, they are students of human nature. The things they do to win their victim's confidence and trust are almost mechanical, as illustrated in these examples:

- o *In a North Jersey case, the con artists rented a beautiful office, hired a British secretary, leased a Mercedes-Benz, and had a beautiful brochure printed—all to sell charter memberships in a health club that was never going to be built.*

- o *In an investment scam in the 1990s, the con artists first got a few Hollywood stars to invest in tax shelters, then used their names to pull in other investors.*

- o *In the famous salad-oil scandal of 1963, the Allied Crude Vegetable Oil Refining Corporation obtained huge loans secured by its soybean-oil inventory, which consisted of a few feet of oil floating on top of huge vats of water (again, I am sad to report, in my native northern New Jersey).*

Each of these cases shows what some people, probably most people, will trust: big-name third-party references, spiffy badges of success, visible "evidence" that something is true, and the fact that most people do business legally.

In Chapter 6 we will look at ways of establishing trust as you engage the persuadee. At this point, I just want to raise the issue of trust and root it in legitimate belief and rigorous preparation on your part, while pointing out that you still have to have certain things in place and give people certain cues if they are going to believe you and trust you.

## Rehearse, Rehearse, Rehearse

You must arrange your mental state and order your emotions so that you appear confident and reasonable to your persuadee. How do you inspire confidence? Try practicing what you will say into a tape recorder, in front of a mirror, or in front of someone else who can give you constructive criticism.

Here are five things to rehearse:

**Your greeting and statement of who you are:** Make this straightforward, at least for now: "Hello, I'm Tom Gorman, and I'm calling to ask you if you've ever thought of writing a business book, or getting one written, based on your business. Because I think there may be a book in your business."

**The tone, timber, and cadence of your voice:** Most people talk in too high a register, espe-

## REHEARSAL AGENDA

- Greeting and opening

- Voice qualities

- Initial request

- Persuadee's position

- Answers to objections

cially when they are nervous. In fact, many people talk in a higher-than-natural register much of the time. Speak in your natural register and at a reasonable pace.

**Your initial request:** Make your initial request reasonable, easy, and non-threatening. I say something along the lines of, "I'd like a few minutes to hear your ideas on the matter, and to broach a couple of ideas of my own, either now, if this is a good time, or another time in the next several days."

**Put yourself in the persuadee's position:** Try to gauge the initial response and the initial form the resistance might take, and anticipate the objections you're likely to hear.

**Rehearse answers to objections:** The actual ones you will hear may be different, but preparing yourself will help you to answer their objections more clearly. You might also rehearse phrases you'll use to secure agreement, for example, "I'd like us to take the next step. How comfortable would you be doing that?"

At this point you are mainly persuading yourself of the legitimacy of your approach and request. Most people find that writing down what they are going to say makes it real and reasonable.

Rehearsing makes it even more real, and if it doesn't seem reasonable to you then, it certainly wouldn't if you were talking with your perusadee. So this is an opportunity to start building a reasonable case as you build your confidence.

## People Take You at Face Value

You hear a lot about people's cynicism and lack of belief in their fellow man. I'm here to weigh in on the other side. Most people are incredibly open, accepting, and unsuspicious of other people. And that includes me. If a guy's walking around in my office building in a brown shirt and pants, I figure he's a hardworking UPS man. If a woman calls me on the phone and says she's a financial planner, I believe her.

> You miss one hundred percent of the shots you don't take.
> —Wayne Gretzky, 1999 NHL Hall of Fame Inductee

We all do the same. There are too many people out there for us to second-guess every one of them. So you can rest assured that even if you feel like a total fraud on the inside, on the outside if you look, sound, and act like a reasonably intelligent individual who is approaching someone in a reasonable manner, that's what they will assume you are. So in your mental preparation, remind yourself that people take one another at face value.

## Dealing with Rejection

One of the most important parts of persuading yourself that you can be persuasive is to deal with your attitude toward rejection. It's a problem for most of us. Actually, rejection isn't the problem; fear of rejection is the problem.

We fear rejection. We fear the word "no." We fear being in a position where we can be refused, a position of less power relative to the persuadee.

Like most of us, I've had difficultly dealing with rejection, so, I've come up with rules that help me deal with it:

**Rule #1:** Nothing ventured, nothing gained. Yes, it's an old saying, but I've taken it to heart. If you don't try, you guarantee that you'll fail.

**Rule #2:** I owe it to others to try. If I have a proposal that might benefit the other party, I actually owe them the opportunity to hear it. If they reject it, that's their decision.

**Rule #3:** Rejection isn't going to kill me—or anyone else. People trying to persuade others risk feeling bad for a couple of minutes or hours. It's not what most of us think of as dangerous work.

**Rule #4:** I am not my proposal. It's the proposal that's being rejected, not my humanity or my hopes, dreams, and life's work.

**Rule #5:** I know what I'm talking about. I always know whom I'm approaching, why I'm approaching them, what's in it for them, what's in it for me, and how I'm going to proceed.

**Rule #6:** I have the right to ask, and they have the right to say no. This is the way it's done.

**Rule #7:** I will find a way. Every "no" gets me closer to "yes." When I find out what I'm doing wrong and fix it, acceptance will eventually replace rejection.

Many bright and talented people drive down the road of life in first or second gear because they fear rejection. Their failure to use all the power at their disposal hurts them far worse than anyone's rejection could. Like the man said, "If you don't ask, you don't get."

## What's My Line?

On my first few days as an executive recruiter, I was astonished to find that people believed me when I called and said, "Hello, this is Tom Gorman and I'm an executive recruiter focused on the banking industry." The day before, I'd been in marketing at one of the banks. Now I'm saying I'm an executive recruiter, when I barely knew a thing about it. Yet from the very first day, people believed me.

## Give Yourself the Benefit of the Doubt

When you persuade someone to do something, often they are giving you the benefit of the doubt. They have doubts, or they would grant your request right off the bat. I'm asking you to give yourself the benefit of any doubt that you may have about your ability to persuade.

Appearances are not held to be a clue to the truth. But we seem to have no other.
—Ivy Compton-Burnett

"

IN PREPARING FOR BATTLE
I HAVE ALWAYS FOUND THAT PLANS
ARE USELESS, BUT **PLANNING
IS INDISPENSABLE**.

"

—Dwight D. Eisenhower
(U.S. President)

# Planning to Persuade

One of the best ways to improve your persuasive skills is the one that improves any skill: planning. Planning brings the future into the present so that you can shape the future more to your liking. While planning won't make the future exactly as you want it, it will help you make it closer to what you want. Also, by anticipating the future, you can be prepared, or at least more prepared, to deal with whatever actually happens.

Whatever you plan, the person you are trying to persuade will respond in whatever manner they want, and often in unanticipated ways. However, their response will be some version of yes, no, or maybe, and you'll be better able to marshal the right appeals and reasons if you've thought things through beforehand.

Planning to persuade involves research and strategy. Your research is guided by your strategy—by whom you need to persuade and what you need to persuade them of—and your strategy is guided by your research—by what you learn and how that new information affects your plan. Your strategy determines your

**Take Action**
*If you don't currently follow
an industry, pick one that
you are interested in and
start doing so. I followed
banking for years, and now
follow book publishing and
the movie studios. Following
an industry's key companies,
executives, and develop-
ments tunes your mind and
helps you as an investor.*

need for information, and as you gather information, you modify your strategy accordingly. In this chapter we'll look at ways of conducting research and developing a strategy.

# Do Your Homework

Given the Internet, research has never been easier. It requires no expertise to enter words into a search engine, examine the results, and read up on a person or subject.

The Web doesn't cover every person and subject, nor is the information always accurate and useful. But you can learn something about many people and most subjects by using the Internet.

Here are some examples:

- If you want to approach a potential client or employer—or any organization for any reason—you can learn about its business, managers, history, locations, and size from its Web site, and from things that have been written about them in other sources you can locate on the Web.

- If you want to sell an article or a book proposal, you can research the online version of many magazines and journals to see what they publish, or review the publishers' catalogs to see who yours is right for; many Web sites *provide the names of editors and provide guidelines for making electronic and hardcopy submissions.*

o *If you want to approach sources of funding, such as the Small Business Administration or a venture capital firm, you can find out about the kinds of loans they offer or the kinds of companies they invest in.*

o *If you are approaching a specific individual, you can learn about his former employers, published work, and even personal background, and perhaps find something you have in common.*

## RESEARCH RESOURCES

o *Search engines*

o *Company reports and press releases*

o *Articles and news items*

o *Alumni and membership information*

Web sites also often mention ways in which the outfit prefers to be approached. Many provide online mechanisms for applying for jobs, submitting proposals, and so on. I am not saying that you should always use them, but they are there. The reason not to use them would be to stand out from the crowd, but be careful. Approaching someone in ways that they don't recommend (as in "no phone calls, please") can backfire.

You can learn a tremendous amount about organizations and individuals on the Web that can help you get a sense of them. Just don't get carried away by the false sense of familiarity that this sort of research can sometimes create. Keep everything businesslike and reasonable.

## What Do You Need to Know?

The key issues are: which information will help you, how can you find it, and how can you best use it? I noted that your strategy will determine your information needs, and your information will help you modify your strategy. But where do you start?

## Targeting, Shotguns, and Rifles

Marketing people employ two overall approaches to locating potential customers: the shotgun and the rifle shot. The shotgun approach covers a lot of ground and depends on the numbers game. Believers in this approach feel that spreading your efforts widely or putting out enough feelers will generate some percentage of hits. Mass marketing via direct mail to huge lists, and mailing your resume to hundreds of companies are examples of using the shotgun approach.

The rifle-shot approach calls for selecting a few targets carefully and putting more effort into hitting each one. You carefully select potential persuadees, cultivate them more

**shot•gun app•roach**

1. Broad coverage and many contacts
2. Low percentage of hits
3. Mass mailing is an example

**rif•le-shot app•roach**

1. Narrow coverage and few contacts
2. Cultivates deeper relationships
3. Focused sales efforts are an example

gradually, and get to know their needs and motives. Marketing efforts directed toward several highly desirable customers, and job searches focused on a few organizations that you really want to join are examples of using the rifle-shot approach.

Each approach has its pros and cons. The shotgun approach has the advantage of broad coverage and typically involves less effort than more precise targeting. On the downside, it relies on the receiver to make the next move and involves greater out-of-pocket expense. You throw a lot of messages out and count on recipients to respond.

The rifle-shot approach delivers your message to someone more likely to be interested. In this approach, you devote more effort to researching each target. You develop more information and rely less on receivers' willingness to respond. Instead of hoping people respond to you, you engage them in a conversation, even if it's a bit one sided at first.

So the shotgun approach is a more passive way of locating people to persuade. That's a benefit for those who don't like approaching strangers, which is why so many people use it. There's less direct rejection in the shotgun approach, yet I believe the rifle-shot works better in most instances when you need to find people to persuade.

## Which to Use?

If the shotgun and rifle-shot approaches each have their pros and cons, which should you use in doing your research and developing your strategy? It depends on the nature of your mission and, to a lesser degree, on your personal preferences. If your mission is to persuade thousands to buy your new shampoo, then the rifle-shot approach could take you a lifetime. If on the other hand, if you need to persuade one outfit to hire you or buy your screenplay, why would you need a shotgun approach?

Of course, you might prefer a shotgun approach, such as direct mail in selling or mailing hundreds of resumes in a job search, because it lowers your exposure to direct rejection. As mentioned previously, the shotgun approach tends to cost more money, but it takes less time. Rifle-shot approaches, such as in-person sales efforts or job searches focused on just four to six companies, are more active approaches. They tend to cost less money but consume more time and expose you more directly to rejection.

## Combining the Two

Actually, people get good results by combining elements of the shotgun and rifle-shot approaches. For instance, in the shotgun approach, you benefit by defining a target market, even if you are trying to persuade millions. (For more on targeting markets and audiences, see the book *Innovation* in this series.) Similarly, in the rifle-shot approach, you benefit by choosing several receivers from a larger population of potential persuadees.

## Consider Gun Control

The shotgun approach has become less effective over the past two decades because it's been overused. In that time, average direct-mail response rates have fallen from two percent to less than one percent. Telemarketing was so overused that Congress created the national Do Not Call list in 2001. Shotgun approaches tend to be unfocused and wasteful. So consider targeting people carefully and using the rifle-shot approach.

Here's an example: When I graduated from business school, I wanted to be hired by one of the loan-officer training programs at one of the major commercial banks in Manhattan. My first step was to find the names and headquarters locations of all the banks in the city. I researched about eighteen banks, even including one head-quartered on Long Island. That was the shotgun part.

My research, which included reading the banks' annual reports and newspaper articles, and talking with people in banking, winnowed my list down to five that I really wanted to join—and three favorites.

I hit each of those banks with a rifle-shot approach, sending a carefully crafted letter to the head of the lending division at each of the banks and following it up with a phone call.

Now, someone else may have sent out resumes and cover letters to all fifteen of these banks, or to the top fifty or one hundred banks in the country. Maybe that person would have obtained interviews and job offers from one or more of those banks. I'm not saying the shotgun approach doesn't work. I'm saying that I prefer the rifle shot in most instances, and have generally found that it works best for me.

**ann•u•al re•port**

1. Presentation of a corporation's financial performance over the past year

2. Report that all companies that issue stock to the public must file with the Securities and Exchange Commission every year

## A Research Plan

In any research you usually—but not always—proceed from the general to the specific, from masses of data to pieces of data. Specific knowledge enables you to approach specific people with specific messages. As you will see in Chapter 5, specifics get people interested in your message.

In any situation in which you want to gain access to and persuade someone,

52

you want to first define your parameters, then get specific. This means gathering broad information on many possibilities, applying criteria based on your wants and needs to those possibilities, then gathering information on the possibilities that meet your criteria.

Here is a five-step process that I've used many times to research and target potential employers, prospects, and other people to persuade.

## Step 1. Define Your Wants And Needs, And Set Your Criteria

Start with what you want to do, and what you are going to need to do it. Focus on your actual wants, not what you think you should want. Again, it's hard to persuade someone of something that you feel iffy about. Your wants and needs are your wins, and they'd best be motivating. We'll deal with the persuadee's wins later.

These wants and needs become your criteria for choosing persuadees. You have to define what you want in order to get it. Just as an example, let's say you want to enter a top-rated graduate school of business in a large city. We'll carry through on this example in later steps.

## Step 2: Research And Define the Universe of Potential Persuadees

Step 1 and Step 2 could actually be reversed, because you *do not* apply your criteria to individual persuadees just yet. Rather, in this step you are defining the overall group or groups of potential persuadees. This is important because if you apply your criteria too soon, you may limit the size of your potential universe of persuadees. This can lead you to missed opportunities, especially when it comes to networking efforts.

To continue with the example of choosing a business school, to define your list of top B-schools you could use the bi-annual list from *BusinessWeek* or the annual list from *US News and World Report*, or a Web-based list. However, if you known which area of business you will focus on—such as marketing, finance, or international business—then ask around to find the best schools in those areas.

## Step 3: Apply Your Criteria to the Universe and Select Possibilities

Once you have your criteria based on your wants and needs, and your universe, you apply your criteria to your list. You may find yourself tempted to ditch one of your key criteria in order to keep a possibility on your short list. You can do this, but do it carefully. When my wife and I chose a part of the country to live in, I was persuaded to ditch my criteria of good weather. What a mistake.

## Organizations Are People

When you approach an organization, you are not approaching a monolithic institution, but rather people who can be persuaded. You must locate the right people, but don't discount anyone in the early states. I've often found contacts with people unrelated to my mission to be extremely helpful. If you engage people, tell them what you're up to, and show them respect and appreciation, they'll help.

The result of this step should be a short list of organizations or people you can persuade. In our example, you would have about five to seven graduate schools of business to apply to (although I know it's common to apply to more).

### Step 4: Research Your Most Attractive Possibilities

Researching attractive possibilities entails getting information that will help you see whether you have the right possibilities on your short list. It also entails getting information that will help you approach, engage, and persuade your receiver. In the process you may discover something that disqualifies this outfit or person from your short list. That's okay, and it's also another reason that your short list shouldn't be too short.

## Step 5: Develop Information and an Approach for Each Persuadee

How much information you need about any potential persuadee depends on the specific situation. I've found that in important situations—those involving a job or big piece of business—I tend to over-research and overprepare. How do I know? Because I consistently use a small fraction of the information I've absorbed about the organization and the people I'm courting.

I continue to overprepare because I believe that being highly prepared gives me the confidence—and the right—to persuade people that I want the job or project and will handle it well. So, "overprepared" is a relative concept. Again, though, I go all-out only when it's worth doing so.

## From Research to Strategy

A strategy is an overarching set of goals along with the methods you will use to achieve them. Those goals and methods dictate the tactics that you'll use at the action level. The goal can be as broad or narrow as you define it. Broadly, it might be to find a job at, sell a proposal to, or obtain funding from one of any number of organizations. Narrowly, it might be to resolve a long-standing problem with a supplier, or to obtain a face-to-face meeting with a specific person.

Let's consider four strategic elements: your goal, receiver, terms, and approach.

## Your Goal

What do you want to persuade the person to do? Define this as clearly as possible. To give me a job or to resolve this problem is not a well-defined goal. To give me a full-time job, on staff, with benefits, as a graphic artist is a well-defined goal. You must have a clear, precise goal as an organizing principle for your persuasive efforts.

### Research Implication

Research the area or discipline around your goal, and get to know the usual channels for reaching your goal. Knowing the usual channels can't hurt—unless you let it limit your thinking. Most information on anything describes the normal channels, and it's good to know what they are. It's even good to use them. But in certain situations, such as finding a job or getting a problem resolved, not using the normal channels can distinguish you while insulating you from competition.

## STRATEGIC CONSIDERATIONS

- Your goal: What do you want?

- Your receiver: Who must you persuade?

- Your terms: What outcome can you accept you?

- Your approach: How will you engage and persuade them?

## Your Receiver

Who do you have to persuade, where, and via what medium? Again, this may be more than one person, but you can only persuade one person, or one set of people, at a time. With that kind of targeting, you can home in on your receiver and take an individual approach.

### Research Implication

Who can help you reach your goal? Think outside the normal and obvious channels here. It took job seekers decades to realize that human resources departments don't hire people (except for others in human resources), and that they should target the hiring authorities. Identify gatekeepers throughout the company. Also identify people who can help you network your way to the people you want to persuade. In terms of the medium, will you approach and persuade them by phone, mail, e-mail, in person, or in some combination? What are their interests, problems, and priorities?

## Your Terms

What represents an ideal, acceptable, and unacceptable outcome to you? In any effort to persuade or negotiate, consider a range of outcomes. Once you are dealing with someone, you can find the ground moving under you. To give yourself some signposts, think through potential outcomes beforehand. For instance, if you want to work at a specific company, your options might include full-time or part-time work, or working on a project basis. Which do you prefer? Which are unacceptable? I am not recommending that you settle for anything. You can define your ideal outcome as your only acceptable outcome, which can be an extremely useful.

> The achievement of your goal is assured the moment you commit yourself to it.
> —Mack R. Douglas (author)

### Research Implications

To the extent that's possible and practical, research your persuadees and their situation. If you know their interests, problems, and priorities, you can better understand what might persuade them. Then you might have a better fix on what you can persuade them to do or offer.

Information is power, and in many negotiations one side holds a real advantage because it knows about its own finances, operations, needs, and motivations, *and* the other side's. Don't deprive yourself of information. Whatever you want to know, someone else knows it. All you have to do is persuade that someone to share that information with you.

## Your Approach and Plan

I plan even brief phone calls in which I intend to persuade someone. This might

### Take Action

*When you are seeking help or trying to solve a problem, list all of the people you know, then list all of the people who could help with this situation or problem. You will probably know some people who can help you directly, and if not, you surely know people who could help you get to those people.*

involve considering the person and their situation, the time of day, and certainly a few bullet points about what I want to say and what their response might be. I put a lot of time and effort into planning meetings and presentations, not because I religiously follow the plan, but because planning is preparing.

### Implications for Research

Your research in the area and on the people you want to persuade will influence your plan, and your strategizing may reveal gaps in your knowledge that send you back to conduct further research. That's how it's supposed to work. You must also research things that will help you shape your approach. For example, if you are approaching an expert about his area of expertise or a company about doing business with them, you should at a minimum have read basic material—say, a few articles or a book on the subject, or the company's annual report. If you seem to lack basic information, you won't inspire confidence and may appear lazy or uninterested, or as if you intended to waste the person's time.

As a result of your research, strategizing and planning, you should feel confident and prepared to engage the persuadee

> You can tell whether a man is clever by his answers. You can tell whether a man is wise by his questions.
> —Naguib Mahfouz (author and Nobel Prize winner)

and present your case. Although I often overprepare, you don't have to. The more experience you have in a situation, the less preparation you will need. If, however, you don't feel confident, ask yourself why, and do all that you can to address that gap in your knowledge or skills.

> **THE BUSINESS OF AMERICA** MUST BE MORE THAN JUST BUSINESS, AND ENGAGEMENT MUST BE THROUGH MORE THAN JUST THE CASH REGISTER.

—David Wu
(U.S. Congressman)

# Master the Rules—and Tools—of Engagement

5

Once you've done your homework and have a plan, it's time to start actually persuading someone. To do that you must first get their attention. Then once you have their attention, you have to keep it.

With a nationwide case of cultural ADD on our hands, that's not easy. Moreover, meetings, travel, voice mail, telephone trees, e-mail, and a lack of receptionists have made getting in touch with the person you are trying to reach—or with any actual person—on any given phone call the exception rather than the rule.

So in this chapter, we look at ways of getting through to the person you want to persuade, capturing their attention, and engaging them. We also explore ways of presenting your request, proposal, or plan in the most attractive manner. But to present anything, you have to break through clutter, and then break through resistance.

## Break Through the Clutter

Clutter has long been recognized as a major problem in advertising, direct mail, and now e-mail. Clutter consists of competing communicators' messages and irrelevant messages. You can't do much about competing messages, except make yours seem as relevant as possible to the receiver. If you've done your research, you should have a fix on your receiver that will enable you to do that.

To make your message relevant, you must somehow appeal to the receiver by keying in on an interest or desire of theirs. Before you can do this, however, you have to get your message to the person you want to persuade. Today, despite the fact that we are all so connected—or perhaps because of it—it is harder than ever to reach the person you want, particularly in large organizations, because of gatekeepers.

### gate•keep•ers

1. Receptionists, assistants, and others who insulate their bosses from unwanted contacts 2. The series of people you have to go through to get to the person who can make a decision 3. Electronic means of avoiding unwanted contact, such as caller ID, e-mail screens, and voice mail

## Dealing with Gatekeepers

To some degree, gatekeepers can bar you from connecting with your persuadee, but getting irritated doesn't help you deal with them.

Gatekeepers—the human, not the electronic, ones—share the same motivations as the rest of us. So, you must convince any gatekeeper that you respect them, their position, and function, and that you are a potentially useful person to know.

Most gatekeepers ask what you are calling about or offer to connect you with the persuadee's voice mail, or both. Unless your communication is personal or sensitive, I believe it's fine to share the nature of it with the gatekeeper. Sometimes, the gatekeeper can tell you when you're after the wrong person and direct you to the right one. Also, you can often interest the gatekeeper in helping you, which I'll cover in Chapter 10.

## Don't Use Ruses

It's tempting to use ruses or lies to get someone to take your call. Don't! I've received calls from salespeople who claimed we had had a great conversation at a conference the previous year, and from others who told me they were calling back like I asked him to six months ago. I knew I never spoke with these yo-yos. Such approaches undermine trust, appear amateurish, and insult the persuadee's intelligence.

## Deliver Your Pitch

When contacted by strangers, most people of substance want them to come to the point quickly. That means conveying basic information to your persuadee, the key points being:

- *Who you are*

- *Why you are approaching them*

- *What you want*

Here is a sample opening:

Hello, this is Wendy Chu, and I'm a customer with a problem that several well-meaning people in your area have been unable to resolve. At this point I'm convinced that they—and I—really need someone at your level to be the tail twister on this one and get it resolved.

Several points about this pitch:

- *It delivers all elements of the basic information: Who you are, why you're approaching them, and what you want.*

- *The message can be delivered in about fifteen seconds.*

- You must speak in a very clear voice and may have to speak at a pace that you feel is artificially slow, particularly if you normally speak quickly.

- This statement mentions and flatters the other person. Wendy expresses confidence in the power of the person she's addressing.

You deliver the statement, and then listen to what the other person says. They give you a canned answer because they were doing something more important, or because they want to avoid a new item on their to-do list. Or perhaps they just can't consider your proposal at this time, or they're the wrong person to be approaching. On the other hand, they may be interested, or at least capable of being interested in what you're saying. You want to ascertain which of these is the case, and you can do that only by listening.

One response you'll often hear is "Go on" or "Tell me more" or "Tell me more about yourself." At that point, explain in more detail who you are, what you are working on, and why you're approaching them. Avoid making this a lecture by engaging the receiver in a conversation. But again, you first must get their attention by pitching the basics in a small, appealing package.

**Take Action**

*For a short, solid primer on pitching see the article "How to Pitch an Idea" by Scott Berkun at www.scottberkun. com/esays/essay38.htm*

## Golden Gatekeepers

If you approach gatekeepers as obstacles and pains in the neck, they'll return the favor. Don't be overly friendly or, worse, patronizing, but treat them as professionals doing a job. Deliver your basic pitch to them as if they were the persuadee, adjusting the wording as necessary. Tell them how you came to call the persuadee, whether through your research, a recommendation, or something on the company's Web site. Talk to them, not at them.

### Voice Mails that Connect

In any voice mail you leave, deliver your basic pitch, but also consider that you don't know when the persuadee is going to check it, and that you have no way of knowing their response.

So, if you can do so gracefully, try to create some sense of urgency in your message. You can do this by mentioning that you may be out of town next week, or—one I like to use—saying, "I know you are busy so I wouldn't waste your time." Be businesslike, and don't ramble and waste space in the voice-mail box.

## VOICE MAIL RULES

- Deliver your basic pitch in a clear voice.

- Leave your name and number at the start and close.

## Try Writing Before You Call

One way to break through the clutter of phone calls, voice mail, and even e-mail is to send a letter to your persuadee. That's right, I'm suggesting snail mail.

How many actual letters do you receive in the mail? Not junkmail or postcards—I'm talking actual letters. Not many, I'll bet.

Am I suggesting adding more to the stream of junk mail already hitting their circular file? No! I am suggesting that you write a letter to your persuadees with one purpose: to get them to accept or return your phone call. Don't try to sell anything in the letter. If possible, send them something of value "to thank them in advance for their time." This might be a copy of a book, article, or white paper of interest to them. If, and only if, the persuadee is worth it, you can even promise to donate $25 to their favorite charity if they give you ten minutes on the phone. Don't expect anything in return for a pen or mug embossed with your company name. That's just more promotional hooey. But you can sometimes create a sense of obligation on the receiver's part with these methods.

## Types of Resistance and How to Deal with Them

Once you break through the clutter and connect with your receiver, you start dealing with resistance. By definition, persuasion aims to overcome resistance, which occurs at three levels.

### Level One: General Resistance

Many people initially resist *any* interruption, distraction, or new information. At this level, they're resisting your proposal when they barely know a thing about it. So there's no reason to take "rejection" personally at this point.

To overcome general resistance, you must capture your receivers' attention *and* engage them. Here's how to go about it:

#### Good Example of Getting Attention on the Telephone

**Persuader:** Hello, I'd like a moment of your time to—

**Receiver:** I'm sorry, now's not a good time.

**Persuader:** I understand perfectly, and I apologize for my timing, but I wouldn't call you about something trivial. When would be a good time for me to call you?

**Receiver:** What's it about?

## What Worked?

The persuader in the example first empathizes with the receiver, then apologizes. Then she points out that she's not calling about something trivial.

If the empathy and apology didn't engage the receiver, which they probably would, he'll almost surely want to know what's so important. If the persuader has a good answer to "What's it about?" the receiver will probably tell her when to call or let her pitch then and there.

## Level Two:
## Specific Resistance

Once you've engaged a receiver and pitched your proposal or plan, they will resist specific aspects or features of it. You can anticipate specific points of resistance if you research your receiver and think through your proposal or plan. Sometimes this isn't resistance, but feedback that tells you you've got the wrong receiver. But when you have the right person, you must be prepared to address points of resistance. Dealing with these points may lead you to modify your proposal to make it more persuasive, but deal with them you must. This book discusses ways of doing that in Chapter 6.

## Level Three:
## Ultimate Resistance

A receiver can listen long and hard to your pitch, but ultimately they have to do more: they have to decide to support or not support your proposal or to support some modified version of it. Ultimately, you must secure a commitment—or a refusal—to act, and this attempt to gain a commitment can generate what I call ultimate resistance.

### "How Are You?" Openings

When someone calls and asks me, "How are you today?" my response, depending on my mood, is, "Busy," "Who's asking?" or "What's it to you?" I know someone is actually concerned about me when they say, "Have I caught you at a good time?" That question acknowledges that they're interrupting what I was doing, and seems polite to me. I'll usually say, "It depends on what this is about," and let them tell me.

Overcoming ultimate resistance is often the most difficult part of persuasion. The final stage of persuasion often involves emotional appeals because it's usually an emotion, typically fear, that holds the receiver back from making the ultimate commitment.

The key to addressing all types of resistance is to anticipate it, expect it, and have ways to overcome it. We'll deal with level-one resistance now, with level-two resistance in Chapter 6, and with level-three resistance in Chapter 7.

Even stupid behavior should be treated intelligently.
—**Chinese proverb**

## Ways of Countering General Resistance

First, ignore any initial crispness, world-weariness, or mild irritation in the persuadee's manner. Quite a few men and women enjoy intimidating other people or putting on an intimidating front, while others use such postures as a hurdle for you to clear. Plus, some people are just ill mannered.

This has nothing to do with you personally, so don't take it personally. Fortunately most people, including those who at first seem crisp or remote, are not rude and can be engaged. How? Here are six ways:

**Humor:** For instance, as a head-hunter, now and then I would say, "Hello, I'm Tom Gorman, and I'm yet one more headhunter trying to entice you away from Citibank." For this sort of thing, you have to be able to size up your receiver very quickly.

**Challenge:** It takes chutzpah to carry this off, but you can actually challenge the receiver to listen to you. "Mr. Hobbstweedle, would you please consider the transaction that I'm trying to engage you in? I'm simply asking for a moment of your time, and in exchange you stand a good chance of learning something new and useful."

**Set Yourself Apart:** Try to distinguish yourself in some relevant way. "I know you get a lot of calls from people who want to get into advertising, but I can assure you that very few have work samples like mine."

**Flattery:** Most people are vulnerable to some form of flattery. "I have researched people this area intensively, and it's clear to me you know more about doing business in Hong Kong than anyone else."

**Pleading:** When pleading, try to give them a reason to listen to you as opposed to simple begging. "Ms. Vanderblock, I've spent two weeks trying to get hold of you, and now that we're on the phone together you won't hear me out? Please give me just two minutes of your time."

**Rescheduling:** If someone who you really need wants to put you off, try not to let them do it permanently. Suggest a specific time that you will get in touch, preferably before or after hours. Then ask if this is the best number for reaching them at that time.

If all else fails, you can always try charm. In fact, you may try it right at the outset.

## What Is Charm?

Charm is an elusive and, today, underrated quality. Charm is about being your best self. It has to do with being positive and upbeat and communicating that, not with the bombast of a motivational speaker, but by your presence. It means taking the daily irritations we all encounter, such as traffic and thunderstorms, in stride. It means being interesting and being interested.

> ### charm
> 1. Presenting your best, most engaging self to the world
> 2. Being interested in other people and able to make them comfortable

Interesting people know what's going on in the world because they follow the doings of their fellow men and women. They are interested in other people.

### Never Get Angry

At all costs, avoid any expression, or even hint, of anger or disappointment at your failure to connect with and engage your targeted persuadee. You will only leave a bad impression. Say whatever you want when you're off the phone or out of his office—but even that's not a good idea. Why let a momentary setback destroy your mood, roil your digestive tract, and color your view of the human race?

"TELL ME AND I'LL FORGET. SHOW ME AND I MAY REMEMBER. **INVOLVE ME** AND **I'LL UNDERSTAND.**

—Chinese proverb

# Chart a Path, Then Lead the Way

Once you've engaged your receiver, you must keep them engaged and move the process forward. This means laying out a persuasive case, identifying potential wins for them and ways of delivering those wins, and building trust all the while. Achieving these aims is the subject of this chapter.

Every process has a beginning, a middle, and an end. This chapter covers the middle of the persuasion process. Your persuadee may raise objections at this stage, but we'll deal with them in the next chapter. In other words, in this chapter we focus mainly on executing the game plan you created before you started to persuade.

## Where You're Headed

Persuading someone can take minutes, hours, days, weeks, months, even years. The key aims during this time are to clearly present what you want the persuadee to do, and provide clear reasons for them to do it. You should also identify the wins for them in doing as you ask, and explain how they will achieve those wins. These may be emotional wins such as recognition, respect, or acknowledgement of their expertise or power. They may be financial wins in the form of future returns for an investor, future earnings for an employer, or future revenue from keeping you as a customer. Of course, there are any of a number of other potential wins.

If you cannot think of any wins for your persuadees, then you may be talking to the wrong people. If they are the right people and you still cannot identify any wins, you may have to promise a future win or do a favor for your persuadee in return. Those are also legitimate tactics. However, first you have to present a persuasive case.

> **case**
>
> 1. Description of a situation or plan of action
> 2. The situation or plan itself
> 3. Reason to act on a recommendation, often called "the business case" in organizations

## The Elements of a Persuasive Case

A persuasive case is, of course, one that works. It's easy to know after the fact whether your case was persuasive. But how can you know beforehand whether you have something persuasive to present?

Here are four conditions that accompany most persuasive cases, regardless of the subject or situation:

- *Trust and credibility*

- *Clear requests*

- *Detailed plans*

- *Strong motivation*

## Trust Is a Must

While your being charming and articulate won't hurt your chances of persuading someone else, it won't help if your persuadee doesn't trust you. The world harbors plenty of charming, well-spoken crooks, and when people discover one, the charm emulsifies into slickness, and articulate language becomes fast talk. So aside from engaging and informing your persuadees, you must establish trust early and continue to build on it in the persuasion process, bearing in mind that trust can be fragile. The moment your persuadee senses dishonesty or selfishness, trust starts eroding.

There are reasons that lying isn't in the large repertoire of persuasive tools. Leaving aside the fact that lying is morally wrong and takes unfair advantage of the other person, if you lie, people usually find out and stop trusting you. At that point the relationship is over, and they will tell other people not to trust you.

If people don't trust you, you cannot persuade them to do anything. If this strikes you as basic stuff, it is, but I bring it up for two reasons. First, many people in business believe that dishonesty is actually part of the game. Indeed, some minor lies are part of the game, and I'll get to that in a moment. But the prevalence of serious lying is why you hear so much talk about ethics in business (not to mention politics). Lying has no part in getting people to buy your products or services, or to come to work for you, or for any other business purpose. Lying destroys companies, careers, and one's character.

## Trust Builder

Once I billed a client for one-third less than our agreed-upon fee for an article. I explained in a letter with my invoice that it took less time than I'd estimated because the article was more similar to an article in their book than I had originally realized. I hadn't set an artificially high price. Rather, I felt my price was high for the work I'd done. They explicitly told me this increased their trust in me.

Second, it's tempting to lie when you're trying to persuade someone, especially when they ask a question. If they ask a question, they are interested and want to move forward, and a negative answer could halt the process. In such a situation, ask why they are asking the question and try to address that negative in your answer. Acknowledging a negative, rather than lying about it or trying to explain it away, will help you establish trust.

If you tell the truth, you don't have to remember anything.
—Mark Twain (author)

## Little Lies

The only lies in business that I condone are the ones that I tell. No, seriously, there are lies that are within bounds, and that most business people have used to influence others. These lies do no harm to the other party or to anyone else, and are usually seen as part of the game. Here are two examples:

- It's common practice to tell someone who's reviewing your proposal (for instance, a book proposal) that several people have expressed interest in it, even if no one has. You are using a third-party endorsement—from a phantom third party, I grant you—and trying to create some sense of urgency. Although most professionals discount this and make decisions by their own lights, this tactic can speed things up a bit. People do the same thing in job searches when they say that they are "talking to a few companies" when they feel lucky to be interviewed by one.

- High-balling your fee or salary request is a common negotiation technique. But be careful, or you

## high-ball•ing

1. Overstating the salary or fee that you will accept in order to set a high opening negotiating point
2. Opposite of low-balling, in which a seller or store advertises an artificially low price to pull in customers, then adds on "extras" to get to the real price

## ma•ter•i•al facts

1. Facts are considered material if the other party may have acted differently if they'd known them
2. Information relevant to the matter at hand and that should be revealed

may price yourself out of the project or job. You must overstate by a reasonable amount, or you will appear greedy and lose the project to someone with more realistic financial expectations. I use this tactic very rarely because I prefer to come up with my price, explain why that's the price, and take it from there.

Misstating material facts is another matter. Lying on resumes about degrees, employers, and responsibilities can get you fired, with good reason. Misstating financial projections, misrepresenting research results, and withholding information on potential risks is always unethical, and often illegal. In sum, if you can't persuade someone of something honestly, then don't persuade them at all.

## Clear Requests

One of the most frustrating things for a persuadee to endure is a long monologue that seems to go nowhere. You have to ask for what you want, and usually, the more specific you are, the better. The exception is when you want the persuadee to come up with the idea or to be the first one to say it, and I'll get to that in moment.

Consider presenting your request in two stages—the first being specific as to what you need, and the second being specific as to how much you will need. If you ask a potential investor for half a million dollars at the start of your presentation, he may blanch. You do have to say you are approaching him for investment funds, but if he asks how much, hold off or quote a large range. Then after you have presented your plan, which is the next step in this sequence, quote a narrow range or the precise number.

Similarly, if you need an extended deadline on a project from your boss, to request an extra month up front may be professional suicide. You may position things better by saying at the outset that you'll need some extra time, then present your plan, and then, after you've presented the justification, request the specific amount of time you'll need. This brings up three tactical points related to requests—overstated requests, modular requests, and asking their opinion—which I want to discuss briefly.

## Overstated Requests

I noted that it's common for people to overstate a fee or salary request. This tactic extends to requests for time, money,

> The object of oratory alone is not truth, but persuasion.
> —**Thomas Macaulay**

***Take Action***
*For a breezy book of anecdotes about arguments read* How to Win Any Argument *by attorney Robert Mayer.*

personnel, materials, and other resources. Overstated requests and high-balling assume a bargaining situation exists in which you must ask for more than you want or need to get what you want or need. Or it assumes that if you get what you request and use less (which obviously doesn't apply to salary requests), you will look good to your boss or persuadee.

This tactic is fraught with problems and opportunities. I know of very few clear guidelines, and they follow:

- In general, avoid overstated requests. If you continually high-ball for resources in an ongoing relationship, you may lose credibility or appear incompetent. At a minimum, you will always receive less than you request.

- Many persuadees want you to justify resource requests, fees, or prices. How do you justify an overstated request without twisting facts? Once you go down that path, you risk your credibility.

- Life being what it is—uncertain, unpredictable, and often tougher than anticipated—overstating can make sense when you're truly unsure of what you will need. In these situations, try to quote a range or an optimistic, pessimistic, and most likely estimate.

**Take Action**

For the fascinating life story of an extremely persuasive (and flawed) individual, read The Power Broker, the Pulitzer Prize–winning biography of Robert Moses by Robert Caro.

Also, resist any temptation to understate your requirements. If you get approval for an understated request and have to go back for an increase, you could look bad or be refused. Be frank about the risks and uncertainties that surround any endeavor and that attend your requests.

## Modular Requests

Modular requests allow you to break large requests into manageable chunks or steps, which you can then discuss as a package, or as individual or incremental requests as needed. This gives both you and your persuadee greater flexibility during the process of persuasion.

### *Ask their Opinion*

As previously mentioned, in a two-stage request, stage one is to tell persuadees what you want or need, and stage two is to tell them how much you want or need. In some situations you can involve your persuadee and get good advice by presenting your case and then saying, "Given what I've presented here, how much time (or money, or other resources) do you think it will take to get this done?"

The situation depends on your relationship with the person you're trying to persuade. The better you know one another

### mod•u•lar

1. Constructed of separate parts that fit together
2. Having parts that comprise units on their own

and the more aligned your interests are in the situation, the more useful this tactic will be. If you don't know each other or your interests are opposed, their answer may be a negotiating ploy.

The most powerful words in the world are: What do you think?
—Dale Carnegie (author)

In situations where your interests are aligned, however, asking the persuadee's opinion can flatter them, involve them, and generate useful information. It could work well with potential investors if you were raising money to fund the start-up or expansion of your business. Yes, you should know how much you need given your business plan, but you could present an array of choices and open the matter to discussion.

### Detailed Plan

Detailed plans mark you as organized, and business people respect others who are organized. People who are organized expect others to be the same and actually become nervous or annoyed in the presence of disorganized people. Even the disorganized would rather be led by someone who's organized. Think about it. I come to persuade you. I have ideas, goals, and requests—but no plan. That's tantamount to saying, "I don't have my act together, and I want you to join me."

The details of planning are beyond the scope of this book (but are covered in the book *Execution* in this series). However, for anything beyond the simplest request for a name and contact information, you must be able at least to outline a plan for your persuadee. Indeed, even if you want only a name and contact information, the person will still probably say, "What do you plan to ask her?" If you answer, "Well, just some stuff," you're toast.

Sometimes this plan may amount to a one-sentence summary of what you will do when the persuadee gives you the go-ahead. At other times this plan may involve multiple, detailed steps, complete with necessary financial and human resources needs, time frames, payback schedules, and even legal documents. Regardless of what level of plan you require, you need to have it in mind or on hand.

## PARTS OF A PLAN

- Goals and tasks
- Resources and people
- Responsibilities
- Schedules and deadlines

### Make Like Moses

Robert Moses, the man who shaped the highway infra-structure of New York after World War II, presented detailed engineering, financial, and operational plans for any project he proposed. He had thought things through so thoroughly that after his presentations the only logical thing for government officials to do was to approve his plans.

## Talk to the Right People

It's surprisingly easy to spend time trying to persuade the wrong person or people. Some people don't want to admit that they don't have the power to grant your request. Others think that they have the power, or the power to persuade the people above them, when they don't. In large organizations, whether you are inside or outside the outfit, people you may not even be aware of can influence decisions. As you'll see in Chapter 10, this reality creates real challenges for salespeople.

> In every place there are 100 people who can say no and only one person who can say yes.
> —Robert Evans (film producer)

That's why, early in any effort to persuade someone in an organization of anything, you must ask who would be involved in the decision and try to get a straight answer. In a job interview, ask who makes the hiring decision. If you're a customer with a problem, find out who would have to approve the solution you want. Don't try to convince people to do something they cannot do.

Don't ignore everyone else. Depending on the situation, you may have to persuade a cast of characters, as is typical in complex sales and serial job interviews. But in other situations—and even in those situations just mentioned—you should focus your best efforts on the decision maker. How do you get the decision maker to take action?

## Strong Motivation

You have to close the deal. If the decision maker trusts you, understands your request, and praises your plan, but doesn't agree to act, then you haven't persuaded him. In a business setting, any number of things can hinder agreement. So it's your job to provide strong motivation to act.

Here are ways to get action or to secure agreement:

**Ask for action.** Explicitly ask the persuadee to do as you request, either on the spot (if you're looking for a contact or resolution to a problem) or within a time frame (if you're looking for a signed contract or for funds to be wired to your account).

**Deal with their doubts.** If they reject your request, that's one thing. You move on to the techniques in the next chapter. But if they agree but express reluctance, or you sense that their commitment is shaky, try to address their doubts if possible.

**Have everything ready to go.** Part of being businesslike and prepared is having everything ready for them to take action if you do secure their agreement. If you are selling something, have the paperwork ready if that's expected. I am not saying that you should always whip out a contract for

**89**

them to sign on the spot, but you must describe the next step, and have them agree to take that step within a certain time frame. Don't leave things vague and hanging.

**Make the next step yours.** It's often useful, if possible, to make the next step yours. That way you may minimize the second thoughts, foot dragging, and bureaucracy that undermine so many efforts in large organizations. Statements that put the ball in your court include, "So, our sales engineer will call tomorrow to set up an appointment with your technical people," and "I'll review this solution with my wife this weekend and I'll call you by the close of business on Monday."

**Make the next step small.** If you are trying to persuade someone to undertake something large or complex, or the situation involves risk to them, bring them along incrementally. Have your request modularized in small enough pieces, or your plan in small enough steps, so the next one's no big deal. (More on this idea is available in Chapter 10.) Remember to avoid asking someone to take a step they're not ready to take, which only generates resistance. On the other hand, if your persuadee says, "I'll think about it," that's not a very concrete next step. Indeed, if you're stuck with that, you might say, "Okay, I'll get back to you on Friday for your thoughts," thus keeping up some momentum and leaving the next action up to you.

**Offer a guarantee, or at least assurance.** If they seem hesitant because they perceive risk, do whatever you can to lessen the perception or reality of risk. Offer a guarantee of some kind—money back if not fully satisfied, free replacement or repairs at their option, or work for a set fee until they are satisfied. Offer them an out at their sole discretion. The vast majority of guarantees are just so-called sleeping pills for clients, allowing them to feel security and even control.

Try to make it as easy as possible for persuadees to take that next step and either agree to do as you ask or move toward that objective. If you cannot obtain their explicit agreement to take the next step, you may have some serious persuading ahead of you.

> **HE WHO HAS LEARNED TO DISAGREE WITHOUT BEING DISAGREEABLE HAS DISCOVERED THE MOST VALUABLE SECRET OF A DIPLOMAT.**
>
> —Robert Estabrook

# Overcoming Resistance and Moving Forward

7

You cannot move a person to a new point of view or plan of action with a snap of your fingers. Persuasion, especially after you've engaged the persuadee, is real work. The real work of persuasion consists of presenting reasoned arguments and emotional appeals with the goal of overcoming the persuadee's resistance to moving to that new point of view or plan of action.

You can't overcome resistance by arguing, let alone by becoming disagreeable (except in rare cases). Arguing and disagreement generate greater resistance. That's the last thing you need because you're already going to encounter level-two and level-three resistance—specific resistance and ultimate resistance—in the normal course of events. In this chapter, we examine the tools for dealing with these levels of resistance. In the next chapter, we look at ways to secure final agreement to your proposal, position, or plan.

## TO DEAL WITH RESISTANCE

- Act like it's part of the process, because it is.

- Try to uncover the reasons for it.

- Address specific resistance with logic.

- Counter ultimate resistance with emotion.

## Reasons versus Excuses

Recognizing resistance when you see it is easy, but your analysis can't stop there. You must also understand why the persuadee is resisting. That's not always easy.

Suppose you're trying to persuade someone to join you for a swim in the ocean, and they don't want to admit that they can't swim. They'll say there's an undertow when there isn't. They'll say the water's too cold when it's not. They'll say they just washed their hair when you both know they can wash it again. They'll say they have to wait an hour because they just ate a couple of hot dogs, and then an hour from now they'll eat a couple more.

If they would just admit that they can't swim, they would save you and themselves a lot of trouble. You could drop the matter, teach them to swim, provide a flotation device, or settle for wading in a tide pool. But for whatever motives, they won't tell you the reason and instead make excuses.

A reason is an actual barrier in the situation or in the persuadee's mind to doing what you suggest. If someone can't swim, they can't join you for a dip in the ocean. If someone has no money and bad credit, they can't buy your pricey product. In contrast, an excuse is an artificial barrier that the persuadee erects to resist your suggestion, argument, or appeal. An excuse is not necessarily a lie, because the persuadee may well believe it. But it's an artificial, rather than actual, barrier.

## Learning about Barriers

To deal with barriers, you must uncover the real reasons for someone's resistance, as opposed to their excuses for not moving forward. You can best do this by establishing rapport with your persuadee and creating an interchange rather than an interrogation. This means putting your persuadee at ease as you present your pitch and supporting arguments, and throughout the process.

***Take Action***
*To learn about cost-benefit analysis and other analytical tools see my book* The Complete Idiot's Guide to M.B.A. Basics.

## Handling Resistance

I recommend that you generally counter level-two (specific) resistance with rational appeals, and level-three (ultimate) resistance with emotional appeals. You'll recall that specific resistance takes the form of objections to specific aspects or requirements of your proposal or plan. Ultimate resistance, which is resistance to final agreement, may also be based on logic, but is often based more on emotion.

However, either specific or ultimate resistance can be driven by logic or emotion. I'm simply defining specific resistance as mainly rational, and ultimate resistance as primarily emotional. Here are statements that indicate the various levels of resistance:

## *LEVEL ONE— GENERAL RESISTANCE*

- *"I don't want to."*
- *"I'm too busy."*
- *"Who are you?"*
- *"Not now!"*
- *"It's not our policy."*

## *LEVEL TWO— SPECIFIC RESISTANCE*

- *"I have other priorities, and this isn't that important."*
- *"We've tried this before, and it didn't work out."*
- *"It's too expensive."*
- *"I can do this myself."*
- *"We don't have time for all these steps."*
- *"I'm assuming all the risks here."*
- *"This doesn't meet my needs."*

○ *"The cost-benefit analysis doesn't support this."*

## LEVEL THREE— ULTIMATE RESISTANCE

○ *"I really can't go through with this."*

○ *"I could damage my reputation/company/future."*

○ *"I don't feel comfortable moving forward."*

○ *"I'm afraid I just can't."*

○ *"I don't know you well enough."*

○ *Stalling, either verbally ("It's still in committee") or nonverbally (not returning calls).*

> ### cost-ben•e•fit a•nal•y•sis
>
> **1.** Totaling and comparing the costs and benefits of a decision **2.** Method of making a decision or choosing an alternative based on whether its benefits outweigh its costs

### Use Logic to Deal with Level-Two Resistance

Specific resistance should be met with rational appeals and logical arguments. Specific resistance can often be addressed with emotional appeals, but that can backfire.

Broadly, specific resistance presents reasons and problems that you can address or solve, or that you cannot address or solve. For instance, suppose you sell cars and a customer wants a four-cylinder model. If you can demonstrate that your six-cylinder model delivers the benefits they desire, you may be able to persuade them to buy it. However, if your dealership doesn't sell hybrid cars, and your persuadee firmly insists on a hybrid, you stand no chance of persuading them to buy one of your cars.

In general, it's best to deal with specific resistance with specific tools. Simple contradiction is not one of those tools, but complex contradiction is. In other words, when you contradict a logical objection, you cannot simply tell the persuadee that he's wrong. You have to show him that he's wrong. How? Here are the specific tools:

- Use clarifying questions

- Minimize the problem

- Cite examples and facts that defuse the problem

### Use Clarifying Questions

When your persuadee raises an issue, ask for clarification with a question relevant to his or her statement. Or use one of the following questions:

## USE THESE KEY PHRASES

- "That's true in some cases, but let's look at this case."

- "It's also good to consider _____."

- "Here's what causes the situation you're worried about."

- "Here's what the numbers say, and I believe they apply here."

- *"Why is that?"*

- *"In what way?"*

- *"How often?"*

- *"Under what circumstances?"*

- *"Toward what end?"*

- *"Can you give me an example?"*

- *"Tell me more about that."*

A question from you serves several purposes. First, it buys you time to assess the statement and formulate a counter-argument. Second, it elicits more information, which helps you clarify the nature, source, and importance of the objection. Third, it keeps the persuadee talking, which usually makes the issue still more specific, and thus easier for you to address.

## Minimize the Problem

You can often actually minimize a problem for the persuadee by shouldering more of the effort, expense, or risk that's creating the problem. For instance, if you want to set up an appointment to interview a persuadee on the phone and she resists because she's busy, tell her you're willing to call anytime, anywhere, and that you'll be totally prepared. You'll do whatever it takes to make it completely convenient for her. The same tactic can work if you're trying to set up a meeting.

You can often minimize a problem by noting how little time, effort, or expense it involves compared with something else. This is a standard tactic in sales. When a salesperson says the annual fee at, say, a gym, costs less than your daily coffee and pastry, he could be talking about more than $1,000 a year. But it sounds like less. This tactic also positions the salesperson to present logical arguments, such as, "Isn't your fitness and health worth at least as much as your coffee and pastry?"

## Problems Are Part of It

Take problems in stride, or your persuadee may think he's raised a major issue. For instance, mention that the issue often comes up. "Yes, lots of people raise that point, but it's not a big deal and I'll tell you why." This acknowledges that the point comes up, but rarely stops things from moving forward.

Another way to minimize the problem is to agree that it is a problem, but to note that everything has a problem associated with it. Even doing nothing can pose a problem. Or you can point out that the problem is quickly overcome by most people. This latter tactic tends to work well in situations that involve change or training. By the way, in sales, assisting people with changes or training can minimize the problem and generate revenue.

## Cite Examples and Facts that Defuse the Problem

Even when a persuadee raises a specific problem, he'll probably lack the facts that you have on hand. Examples, and facts work well because you are using reasoned arguments to counter reasoned objections. For instance, suppose you sell laser and radar detectors, and your prospect is concerned that they may be confiscated by the highway patrol in his state. You might see that as fear, and it could be, but I would see it as the customer not wanting to lose his investment. If you say that your company offers a full money-back guarantee if the police discover and confiscate the detector, and that you have only had to pay on two such claims in more than 10,000 sales of the product, that's pretty compelling data.

When examples and facts do not overcome rational objections, either of two things may be at work. In the first category, the persuadee may not trust you or your information, or he may think you're cherry-picking your examples and facts. Therefore, you must admit facts that run against your argument into the conversation, but also cite highly respected sources for your information. Second, the persuadee may have a submerged emotional objection, in which case mere logic usually won't carry the day. I say "usually" because if the emotions aren't particularly strong or deeply held, facts may open the way to new thinking.

Use the preparation stage to research and organize the factual information you'll need in your effort to persuade. Your mastery of the facts will reassure the persuadee as much as the facts themselves.

> Everyone is entitled to his own opinion, but they're not entitled to their own facts.
> —Daniel Patrick Moynahan (U.S. Senator)

## Risks of Using Emotion Against Reason

You can often override specific resistance with emotional appeals rather than reason, but doing so poses risks. An alert persuadee might think his logical arguments must be sound if you don't address them. You can also erode trust by playing on emotions when you should be using reason. Or, the persuadee may think that you see him as too dumb to grasp logical arguments. That could insult him or lead him to wonder whom he's dealing with and what he's getting into. Finally, many persuadees view emotional arguments as needless moralizing, and respond with anger.

Also, using emotional arguments to counter logical resistance can amount to intellectual dishonesty. The costs of this dishonesty are obvious in the U.S. political arena, where logical, fact-based arguments have been largely abandoned in favor of emotional appeals. This has usually been the case in politics, of course, because it's easier to offer an emotional appeal than to develop and explain rational arguments. Moreover, many issues are complex, and most people can be led by their emotions, especially in groups. However, both the right and the left have used and misused emotional appeals to the point where reasoned arguments are now rare. As a result, much of the populace now feels apathy, anger, frustration, or cynicism when they think about politics.

## Politics as Usual?

Using emotional appeals to override logic usually won't work on individuals as well as groups. Savvy individuals often lose respect for persuaders who rely on emotion. Yet even tens of millions of people can come to feel that a persuader who relies on emotion is either out to bamboozle them, as in the case of Bill ("Slick Willy") Clinton, or cannot reason clearly, as in the case of George W. ("Dim Son") Bush.

Whenever possible, try to meet specific resistance with logical arguments and keep emotional appeals in reserve.

## Use Emotional Appeals to Deal with Ultimate Resistance

You can't counter emotional resistance by denying the persuadee's feelings. Indeed, if you tell persuadees that they're not feeling what they're feeling, they'll resent it. It's equally useless to deny the legitimacy of their feelings, for instance by saying, "You shouldn't feel that way," or "Nobody else feels that way." Their point is that they feel that way, and that's the point that you have to address.

### The Reflective Technique

One of the best tools I've found for dealing with others' emotions is the reflective technique. It's a stock tool in psychotherapy, counseling, and other helping professions, and it's useful in many communication situations, including persuasion. With the reflective technique, you validate the other person's emotions by acknowledging what they are feeling without judging whether they should or shouldn't feel that way.

Here is an example:

**Party #1:** When my husband doesn't leave a tip in restaurant I want to slink out of the place.

**Party #2:** That must be embarrassing for you.

**Party #1:** It sure is. The last time we were out he . . .

And here is an example regarding persuasion:

**Party #1:** I guess I'm just afraid to make this move.

**Party #2:** It's always scary to make a change.

**Party #1:** That's true. But what scares me most about this is . . .

### Reflect Rather than Correct

With the reflective technique you recognize a person's feelings without judging them, and that builds trust. It lets them know that it's safe to express their feelings to you. That sense of trust and safety lets them know they can talk openly with you, which in turn enables you to learn about their real emotional barriers to being persuaded.

## re•flec•tive tech•nique

1. Restating someone's feelings in similar words and empathizing with them

2. Tool of counselors that validates clients' emotions without agreeing with or denying them

For instance in the example previously, if Party #1 (the persuadee) says that what scares him most is a move to a new town, you can mention how friendly the new area is and that it's a growing area with lots of recent arrivals. If what scares him is revealing confidential information about his company to you, you can suggest that you sign an agreement to hold all information confidential, or that you supply references who can vouch for your honesty.

The reflective technique elicits information because, quite simply, it prompts you to be a good listener. Good listeners ask questions, hear the answers, try to understand how the other person feels, and express empathy. By the way, if this seems like manipulation to you, you may also agree that the world could use a bit more of this kind of "manipulation."

**Take Action**
*At the next opportunity you have, when someone talks about a situation or feeling, use the reflective technique. Instead of judging them or trying to solve their problem, express empathy, and watch the direction the conversation takes.*

## Building a Bridge

After you understand how the person feels (and they do, too) it's time to build a bridge to a new feeling and, if possible, lead them across it. You must do this with sensitivity, good timing, and reasonable objectives. You must be sensitive to depth of emotion that's driving that resistance. Good timing means knowing where the persuadee is in the process and not pushing them to take steps they're not ready to take. As to reasonable objectives, don't expect instant, wild-eyed enthusiasm—although that would be nice. Usually, you need only aim to replace a negative, resistant feeling with a positive, forward-thinking one.

Here are is an example of bridging:

> **Persuadee:** I just don't feel comfortable giving you that information.
>
> **Persuader:** I wouldn't want you to do anything you're not comfortable with. Instead, I'd like to understand your discomfort and maybe help you become comfortable with this idea, if that's possible. What do you think might make you feel more comfortable with it?

In this example, you want to get the *persuadee* to talk about becoming comfortable or moving forward. If they tell you what would make them comfortable or about the risks of not going along with you, they're starting to think in more positive terms.

If they can't be specific, try to suggest some potential solutions. For instance, the example, you could say, "Would you be more comfortable if I were to sign a formal confidentiality statement?" or "Would you feel more comfortable if someone you trusted endorsed this deal?" Follow up these closed-end questions with more open-ended ones such as "What else might improve your comfort level?" or "What other risks might arise?"

### *Make It Attractive*

When you bridge to a new feeling, make it attractive to the persuadee. Most people overcome resistance, fear, and inertia by envisioning good outcomes and improved circumstances as a result of taking action. Really persuasive people paint a vivid picture of the post-persuasion situation. Here are some examples of such a picture:

> **Persuader:** Think about it: You will have helped someone out, someone who won't forget it, and launched a young architect on a successful career.
>
> **Persuader:** By making this move now, your company will avoid higher costs down the road *and* be far ahead of competitors still stuck in the 1990s.
>
> **Persuader:** Yes, it might disrupt your workday a little, but think of the smiles on the faces of those kids when they get off the bus for a week on a real farm. Long after they leave your place, they'll remember that week. I'll bet you'll remember it, too.

Some persuaders are shy about using emotional appeals. That puts them at a disadvantage when they're dealing with the persuadee's emotions.

It takes emotion to move the person across the chasm of their doubts and fears. It even sometimes takes a bit more, as you'll see in the next chapter.

" I WOULD RATHER TRY TO PERSUADE A MAN TO GO ALONG, BECAUSE **ONCE I HAVE PERSUADED HIM, HE WILL STICK**. IF I SCARE HIM, HE WILL STAY JUST AS LONG AS HE IS SCARED, AND THEN HE IS GONE. "

—Dwight D. Eisenhower
(U.S. President)

# Getting Agreement and Closing the Deal

8

The object of overcoming resistance is to move the persuadee to undertake your plan, implement your proposal, or support your position. Persuasion is conversing with a purpose, and in business and most other aspects of life, the purpose is to move people to act.

## Why Gaining Real Agreement Can Be Hard

You may think you're doing really well in the persuasion process, but at the end find that you didn't achieve your goal. This can happen for several reasons:

> ○ *Some persuadees go along with you just to be agreeable or to avoid hurting your feelings. They agree when it doesn't cost them anything, but when they have to act as you suggest, they part company and sort of hope you don't mind.*

- *Many persuadees use agreement as a form of resistance. They want to avoid argument, contradiction, and evasion—although they're practicing a form of the latter. Indeed, most sales professionals would rather field prospects' objections than have them agree with everything they say.*

- *Some persuadees genuinely do agree with your arguments, but not to the extent that they would expend time, money, energy, or other resources on the proposition.*

- *You may have been more focused on your performance as persuader than on your persuadee's responses. Always stay tuned to your persuadee and check your progress toward your goal, which is not to perform but to persuade.*

- *Some persuadees are picking your brains while you think you're persuading them. They're in their information-gathering process rather than your persuasion process. This can be depressing because, in a sense, the persuadee has used you.*

Getting someone's commitment to take action is usually the most difficult step in persuasion.

It is impossible to persuade a man who does not disagree, but smiles.
—**Muriel Spark**

## Know Where You—And They—Are

To avoid the sad surprises just described, you must read your persuadee accurately. Engaged persuadees exhibit the following behaviors:

**They ask questions.** If your persuadee doesn't ask good, relevant questions, he's not really engaged in the process.

**They share information.** Certainly in sales situations, but also when you seek a commitment regarding a charitable effort, political cause, or business matter, persuadees should be telling you about their experiences, needs, and resources.

**They give you their attention.** If they take phone calls, check e-mail, or raise irrelevant issues, you have probably failed to engage them, even if they agreed to meet with you or take your call.

**They are straightforward with you.** If someone clearly indicates that they're not open to persuasion, take them at their word. These people take things seriously enough not to waste your time and theirs.

Many people feel they are "on" when they deliver an energetic pitch or presentation. A better measure of your performance is the persuadee's level of engagement.

## Handling Rude Behavior

I've found that unless rude behavior—interruptions, preoccupations, asinine remarks, and the like—seems deliberately directed toward me, it's best to ignore it at first and then, if it persists, question it. Some people are rude without knowing it, while others are out to show you how unimportant you are. In the first case, when you point it out, they will probably apologize and stop; in the second, they will see that you stand up for yourself, and will probably (but not necessarily) apologize and stop.

To point out rudeness you can give a disapproving look, gently shake your head no, or both, or say, "I'm sorry, that doesn't work for me." One sure-fire way out is to get up and leave while saying, "I'll come back at a better time."

You will occasionally meet people who are deliberately rude or out to play ego or head games. Three words: Life's too short. Just end the conversation, leave their office, or otherwise remove yourself from the situation. If you feel you need

## SIGNS OF ENGAGEMENT

- They ask questions
- They share information
- They give you undivided attention
- They're straightforward

**Capitol Rudeness**

For a defense contractor's market research, I visited a Senator's staffer by appointment. He promptly told me that our research was BS and that he didn't want to participate. I got up, left, called the Senator's chief of staff, and told him what had transpired. The chief invited me back and personally sat for the interview. He had the snotty staffer call me later to apologize, which he did with undisguised contempt (for me, a taxpayer!).

them badly enough to endure rudeness, your problem isn't that you can't handle them. Your problem is that you're inexperienced, you don't think enough of yourself, or your set of potential persuadees is too small.

## Knowing When You're Close to a Deal

I'll talk more about "closing" in the sales sense of the term in Chapter 10. However, a concept from sales known as "buy signals" is useful in any type of persuasion. Broadly defined, a buy signal expresses interest in moving forward, rather than resistance. It usually indicates that you have overcome a point of resistance and are making progress.

Buy signals can be overt or subtle, and of course you handle them differently than you would handle resistance. The problem is that, as a persuader, you can

## buy sig•nals

1. Questions or statements from persuadees that indicate a desire to commit
2. Also known as buy signs

be so immersed in dealing with resistance that you miss or mishandle a buy signal. Here are verbal buy signals you'll hear in various situations:

○ *"How soon would I have to act?"*

○ *"How do you ensure confidentiality?"*

○ *"Whom would I be dealing with besides you?"*

○ *"What else is involved, you know, the fine print?"*

○ *"How do I get started?"*

○ *"What information do you need from me?"*

○ *"If I were to move forward, how soon would I know whether I'm approved?"*

○ *"Can I contribute/pay/invest over time instead of all at once?"*

○ *"When can you/I start?"*

These questions concern the details and ramifications of making a commitment. However, they do not ensure that you have a commitment. Human nature being what it is, people sometimes ask these questions for the heck of it, out of curiosity, or to "be nice" and encourage you.

But buy signals usually indicate real progress. So, what should you do when you hear a buy signal?

## Prompt for Commitment

When you hear a buy signal, the persuadee may be persuaded. There's only one way to find out—respond to the buy signal and then to ask them to move forward. This resembles the bridging tactic covered in Chapter 7, but you are bridging to commitment. Here are four tactics for moving toward final agreement:

**Take Action**

*Visit the site for the Program on Negotiation at Harvard Law School,* www.pon.harvard.edu, *for a huge array of resources on all aspects of negotiation.*

**1.** If the persuadee asks any of the buy-signal questions listed above, answer him and then suggest taking an action related to the question. For instance, if he asks about ensuring confidentiality, say, "I have a confidentiality agreement that I use with all my clients, and I'll send it to you tomorrow morning."

**2.** If the persuadee asks about a barrier or a problem that might stand in the way, say, "If we can get that resolved, can we move forward?" or words to that effect. Then go on to resolve the problem or describe how you'll resolve it, and ask for action.

**3.** When you have presented your major points, say, "How do you feel about this so far?" If he's positive, present the points or ask the questions that must be addressed to finalize things. If he's not comfortable or not interested, ask why, and address his reason or his emotional issue. If you can't address the issue, you may have to move on to your next persuadee.

**4.** After you feel that you've addressed all the persuadee's concerns, say, "Do we have a deal?" If he says yes, confirm the details regarding the next steps, such as what you will do, when he'll see a contract, or where he should send his check. If he says anything other than yes, ask, "What would it take for us to have a deal?" In general, rather than apply high pressure, ask for the green light.

## Getting the Green Light

High-pressure techniques can undermine you as a persuader. The truth is that persuadees can get out of many, if not most, deals, unless they've signed a contract. Even then, in certain situations and in certain states, particularly in areas of sales that are known for high-pressure tactics, such as health-club memberships and used-car sales, the law allows people to undo contracts within a certain time frame.

Similarly, the law recognizes the concept of duress—pressure that negates a contract—if you somehow compel someone to agree to something, or compel him to do something. And persuadees can always stop payment on checks.

So, you must ensure that your persuadee is convinced and comfortable with whatever you've persuaded them to do. One of the best ways to do this is to make it clear that *they* are giving *you* the green light. They are making a decision or taking an action that enables you to make a decision or take action.

The term green light says that you are putting things in motion on the persuadee's say-so. So you can often move things forward by talking in those terms, for example, by saying:

> ○ *"If you give me the green light, I'll have our technician visit tomorrow to define the specs for your system."*

> ○ *"Now that you've given me the green light, tomorrow I'll call the people whose names you've given me."*

Of course, you can convey the idea of moving forward based on their commitment without ever saying the phrase "green light":

> ## high-press•ure tech•niques
>
> 1. Verbally pushing the persuadee to take action
> 2. Demands, deadlines, challenges, criticism, or threats designed to force someone to agree

- "Now that you've made the commitment to support us with these funds, we'll be meeting with our ad agency to mount the next big push."

- "It's settled then: I'll tell the committee that I have your support, which is the final piece in winning their approval."

The point is that you are going to do something now that they are on board. That lets them know that you are counting on them, that the wheels are in motion, and that they can't back down now. It also lets them know that they are dealing with a person of substance. They gave you the green light and you are moving ahead, as you said you would.

I'll discuss dealing with paperwork in Chapter 10, which covers selling and fundraising. For now, I just want to point out that any contracts or agreements that you can get the persuadee to approve—or anything else that signifies a commitment in a tangible way, such as a signed check—will help, provided the persuadee is convinced and comfortable.

## Go for It

It's easy for many of us to remain timid when a display of enthusiasm, desire, or aggressiveness might close the deal. Many a nice guy has marveled at the number of seemingly terrific women who are attracted to aggressive jerks, or at the number of sales that overbearing salespeople rack up, and the theatrics that certain attorneys get away with in court. But many people find those behaviors attractive and even seductive. Why might that be?

It's largely a matter of style and confidence. An aggressive style and confidence tend to go together in many people's minds, especially in the United States. In any culture, it can be hard to resist someone who seems dead sure of themselves. That's confidence. Also, it takes confidence to show emotion. The Casper Milquetoasts of the world are afraid to show emotion because it puts them out there and makes them vulnerable. However, it's that vulnerability, or perhaps the trust in others that vulnerability can communicate, that attracts people.

So, what can the rest of us learn from these alpha persuaders? Not how to act like aggressive, jerky, theatrical blabbermouths, but rather how to understand the persuadee's view of them. Persuadees want to be seduced. They want someone to tap their sense of adventure, or at least recognize that they have one. They want to partner with someone who knows what he wants and goes after it.

## When Were You Desperate?

Think about a time when you had to persuade someone, and did so. Maybe you were in a bad street situation. Perhaps you had to land the project or get that ride to Altoona, or had to resolve a problem or get out of a mess. Recall your mental and emotional state at that time, and the things you said and did when you pulled out all the stops. You can do that again, whenever you want to.

To the extent that you can—in your own way—show emotion and project confidence, you should do so.

## TO SHOW EMOTION

- *Raise or lower your voice*
- *Speak slower or faster*
- *Use hand gestures*
- *Choke up, sigh, or (last resort) cry*

### Define Your Deal Breakers

In any negotiating situation, it's smart to have one or two walk-away conditions, or deal breakers, that you have defined in your prepersuasion planning. I'm not talking about making them up; if you don't have a walk-away condition, then you don't—but you probably do. It might be a demand for a minimum salary or price, a certain delivery date or warranty coverage, a job content or title, or an exclusive versus non-exclusive relationship.

You give yourself leverage when you decide up front that the world isn't going to end, and your self-respect will be intact, if you cannot persuade the other party. Being willing to walk away enables you to persuade with confidence because at one level you don't care if the deal goes south if certain things aren't in place.

You should be frank about your deal breakers as soon as it makes sense. There's no sense in leading people on. However, it can be especially effective in the final stages to indicate that you are willing to walk away if the other party can't or won't meet a certain condition. That condition might be to agree to move forward then and there.

This can be a powerful negotiating strategy, so you must use it sparingly and wisely. If you communicate that you are willing to walk over trivial disagreements or that you don't care about the other party's needs, you're not being persuasive—you're being unreasonable.

Being unreasonable can work if you have the upper hand in the situation; however, you may create lasting resentment because the other party will remember that you exploited the advantage you had. Then when they have the advantage

### Take Action

*Get hold of a copy of* Beyond Reason: Using Emotions as You Negotiate *by Roger Fisher and Daniel Shapiro.*

over you—and life often works that way—they may well take the opportunity to exploit you. As they say, what goes around comes around.

As a closing strategy, being willing to walk often works as a demand for a final answer by a certain deadline or for a certain price, salary, or other condition. This can be construed as "take it or leave it," so don't present it that way. Instead, phrase the demand in terms of your needs ("I really must know by close of business this Friday, or I'll have to withdraw the proposal"). Sometimes, you can soften the demand by laying it off onto someone else ("I want your business badly enough to give you the price you want, but, I'm sorry, I just can't sell that to my chief financial officer").

## Persistent or PITA?

A key skill in obtaining closure is to be persistent without being a pain in the ass (PITA). The line between persistent and PITA can be thin, because in a sense being persistent is being a PITA. So you have to do it in a nice, reasonable way (as much as possible).

This means approaching the persuadee with respect for their position, time, and feelings. You can sometimes win sympathy

## A Walking Baseline

In the 1980s, computer giant IBM wanted an exclusive license to Microsoft's operating system, but CEO Bill Gates persuaded IBM to accept a nonexclusive license. Later Gates told *US News and World Report*, "there were many points in the relationship where we had to walk because they were saying something would be exclusive." How did Bill Gates persuade mighty IBM to accept a nonexclusive license? He was willing to walk if it wasn't.

through light humor ("I'm just making my rounds, checking your temperature at First City Bank") or by acknowledging what you are doing ("Please don't blame me for being persistent, given what's at stake here"). Another way to persist during the process is to continue to state and restate, in various ways, the benefits of your proposal—that is, the benefits to them, not to you.

Never become confrontational or argumentative. Instead just keep calling, voice mailing, and e-mailing to keep gentle pressure on the persuadee. Sooner or later they will give in, tell you it's no-go, or ask you to come back in several months or so. People know they can get rid of you by offering zero encouragement or, failing that, just telling you to stop calling. Thus, they will tolerate some persistence on your part, but if possible you don't want them telling you to get lost. So, try to time your approaches accordingly.

## Silence Is Golden

One of the best techniques to use in persuasion is to ask for something or make a statement, and then shut up. Many, many people make a request or present an idea, and then undercut themselves by adding to it or qualifying it. Some would-be persuaders even add a statement that gives the persuadee an excuse not to answer.

### I, The Persuaded

My literary agent, Mike Snell, stands among the best persuaders I know. He's convinced me to take on several projects I initially rejected, and they've always worked out well. How? Over the years, I've noticed that he never actually contradicts me. He simply restates and elaborates various aspects of his point of view, and keeps doing that unless he hears a "yes" or a firm and final "no."

We do this because we find silence uncomfortable. We don't want to pressure the persuadee. We identify with them and want to relieve their discomfort. But when you're trying to persuade someone, you have a right to ask and they have a right to refuse.

I hate to put it on this basis, but in certain situations the first person to speak loses, in effect. For instance, if in a salary negotiation for a new job you say, "I'd like to come on board, but I don't see how I can do it at that salary," you put the burden of dealing with that on the persuadee. If you say *anything*, you relieve her of that burden. I'm not saying you'll get what you want; I'm saying the burden of dealing with the issue is on her at that moment.

Similarly, if the hiring manager were to say to you, "If you really want to join us, a swing of five thousand dollars in salary shouldn't be that big a deal," and you remain silent, he then has to acknowledge somehow that it is a big deal. Anyway, it's disingenuous for him to say that money shouldn't be an issue in a hiring situation, and he knows it. Your silence simply lets him know that you know it, too. At certain times, you can be most persuasive by saying absolutely nothing.

> Never forget the power of silence, that massively disconcerting pause which goes on and on and may at last induce an opponent to babble and backtrack nervously.
> —**Lance Morrow** (author and *Time* magazine columnist)

### dis•in•gen•u•ous

1. Appearing to be frank and candid when in fact you are not
2. Common posture for people to assume in business dealings

"I NOTICE THAT YOU **USE PLAIN, SIMPLE LANGUAGE**, SHORT WORDS AND BRIEF SENTENCES. THAT IS THE WAY TO WRITE ENGLISH. IT IS THE MODERN WAY AND THE BEST WAY."

—Mark Twain
(author)

# Writing to Persuade

9

Just as you have to speak with people in certain ways to persuade them, so must you write to them in certain ways in order to persuade them. Persuasive writing is so challenging that professional copywriters spend their days crafting print advertising, Web sites, direct mail, e-mails, and product literature to persuade people to come to stores, buy products, and place orders.

Then there is the world of persuasive writing beyond sales. When you write a memo requesting action or proposing a plan, or when you write a complaint to a vendor or a letter demanding money that's owed to you, you are writing to persuade. Even when you are writing just to introduce yourself or to convey information, you are writing to persuade. You want to persuade the recipient to remember you or the information. So in this chapter we examine ways to persuade on paper or by e-mail.

> ## pap•er•less off•ice
>
> 1. Business in which all communications and records are handled by computer
> 2. Yet-to-be realized dream of technologists

## You Can't Avoid Writing

You can't avoid writing, even if you want to. The so-called paperless office may never come to pass, given the laser printer's productivity. Anyway, e-mail is a form of writing, although some debate that point. Moreover, most business people need to see something in writing before they commit to a major decision or action plan.

So if you have to write, do it right, especially if you're writing to persuade.

## Persuading on Paper

To persuade on paper, you don't have to reinvent the spiel. You just have to transfer the basics of persuading in person to paper, with a few refinements. The key difference is that you can't witness your receiver's responses. In fact, you won't even know whether you got their attention. This means that you must present your case, address the resistance that's likely to arise, and ask for action. Here are general guidelines:

○ Get to know your readers through research and putting yourself in their place.

○ Capture your readers' attention in whatever way makes sense. You can be straightforward or mysterious,

**GENERAL GUIDELINES**

○ Know your reader.

○ Capture their attention.

○ Build trust and deal with resistance.

○ Ask for action.

*serious or humorous. But always ad-dress readers in a direct, personal way.*

○ *Build trust by providing useful information, show-ing that you've done your homework, empathizing with them, and supplying examples and* testimonials.

○ *Anticipate points of resis-tance and present logical arguments and emotional appeals that address those points.*

○ *Ask for action after you have made your case. Also, create a sense of urgency and leave the door open for follow-up.*

### test•i•mon ials

**1.** Written endorse-ments or recommen-dations from past or present clients
**2.** Complimentary quotes used with the clients' permission

## Knowing When to Write

Some situations lend themselves to per-suading on paper, and some don't. You have to match the medium to the goal. Some cases are obvious; for instance, when you're selling a big-ticket item or solicit-ing a large donation, you need a personal meeting. For smaller sales and donations, you can use mail, or perhaps e-mail. To enlist someone in a major endeavor, you must meet with them, or at least discuss matters on the phone. To network your way to a solid contact, the telephone may suffice. Complaints to vendors are usually best lodged by phone, but if that doesn't work, writing often helps.

## PERSUASIVE FORMS OF PROSE

- Announcements and requests
- Proposals
- Letters of compliant
- Collection letters

**Take Action**
*For excellent guidelines on business writing, read* Write to the Top *by Deborah Dumaine, president of Better Communications.*

So, the first decision is whether to write. Here are typical situations that call for persuasive writing:

**Introductions:** If you don't know someone, writing to them is one way to get their attention and interest.

**Requests for action:** If you must persuade a lot of people to, say, attend a meeting or promotional event, writing is the way to go.

**Proposals:** Enlisting people in complicated, risky, or long-term efforts calls for a written proposal, even if you'll also meet them.

**Complaint letters:** Writing helps present things coolly and logically.

**Collection letters:** Someone who owes you money might dodge your phone calls, but increasingly demanding letters create a paper trail that becomes hard to ignore.

Let's see how each of these forms of writing can be most persuasive.

## Introductions: Here I Am

The telephone is more personal and interactive than a letter, but most of us dislike making cold calls. As mentioned previously, it's also tougher than ever to reach people you don't know by telephone. So a persuasive letter can turn a cold call into a warm call.

Strive to present yourself as someone the persuadee would like to know, or benefit from knowing (or at least as someone who deserves the courtesy of an answered call or a return call).

## Sample Letter to Introduce Yourself

Dear Ms. Nicholson:

Do you read or rely on information gathered in market research and other business surveys? If you're like most people, you do. And if you're like most senior executives, you feel you are too busy to take part in those surveys.

I'm writing to you because I need your help. (I also have something to offer you in return.) I am the project leader for O'Dell's Operations Executive Survey, which we at O'Dell Research conduct annually. My records show that you haven't participated in this survey, and I want you to reconsider that decision this year.

You are certainly familiar with the challenges facing U.S. manufacturers—cost pressures, global competition, and unpredictable demand, among others. What you may not know is that executives benefit from sharing their concerns about these matters in our annual survey. But the information we supply to executives like you is only as good as the information we obtain from them.

I'll be calling you next week to tell you a bit more about our survey and the benefits of participating. Meanwhile, I've attached a complimentary copy of the executive summary of last year's survey for you. I would appreciate having an opportunity to talk with you next week. Remember, I am only asking only for you to take my call, not to make any purchase or investment.

Thank you for your consideration.
Sincerely,
*Lyle Gray*

## OUTLINE FOR A REQUEST

**Paragraph #1:**

○ Lead with the general request

○ Note the deadline or time frame

○ Mention the overall reason for—and importance of—the request

**Paragraph #2:**

○ Present the details of your request

○ Be very clear about the way to carry out the request

**Paragraph #3:**

○ Anticipate objections and difficulties and defuse them

○ Thank the reader for their help.

This letter approaches the reader in a way that respects their position and time, and asks that they accept a phone call. The writer offers something for free that the reader would probably find interesting. And it mentions the next step—the phone call coming next week—and the desired response, which is that the reader accept the call. A letter like this adds expense to the effort to persuade, but it does increase your contact rate.

## Requests for Action

As a manager or professional you will write memos, letters, and e-mails asking people to attend meetings, provide information, and follow new procedures. But people don't necessarily do what they are asked to do, even by their managers. Sometimes they don't understand the request. Sometimes they don't see the importance of doing it. Sometimes they just don't get around to it.

So you must make any written request clear and persuasive and ensure that it conveys some sense of urgency. Here's an outline for a straightforward request:

## Using Threats and Consequences

Depending on the situation, it can be useful to include a threat or consequence in the memo—at the second or third request.

## Sample Request for Action

**To:** All Managers and Administrative Personnel
**From:** Jim Devon, Manager, Mailroom & Shipping Services
**Re:** Need for Cost-Center Codes on Outgoing Mail

Please be sure your cost-center code is written in the upper right-hand corner on all outgoing mail. We have recently received many pieces of mail without cost centers on them.

While I understand that everyone is busy, we in Mailing & Shipping Services are also busy. The volume we handle does not allow us to put cost-center codes on outgoing mail. When we do have to put cost-center codes on outgoing mail, it slows up both that mail and delivery of everyone's incoming mail.

If you do not know your cost-center code, you can get it by calling me at ext. 653 or Ann Baxter at ext. 311 in Accounting. Thank you in advance for your cooperation.

Notice how the writer acknowledges that everyone is pressed for time, to create common ground. The point that everyone's mail is delayed while the mailroom looks up cost-center codes will not be lost on those who do use their codes. That puts peer pressure on those who don't use the codes. Finally, Jim offers help in case some readers don't know their cost-center codes.

The sample below shows the second request on the cost-center issue. Read this sample carefully because it shows how to use a threat properly.

Be very careful with threats. Never use them in first requests without a very good reason. Always make them sound like consequences, not threats. Be sure you can follow through on the threat, that it is practical, and that you have the authority to make it and to enforce it.

Finally, if you must mention a consequence, link it to what you're trying to accomplish. Don't threaten an unrelated action or something out of proportion to what you're requesting.

### Following Up on Requests

Use the phone to follow up written requests that fail to produce action. No matter how persuasively you write, a memo or e-mail is easier to ignore than a phone call or personal visit. For example, instead of making a third written request, Jim Devon should call the managers of areas not putting cost-center codes on their mail. As a fourth step, he could visit them to discuss it.

### See You in Court

I've gone to small claims court only once. My car was stolen from a service station and later located nearby, drivable but damaged. When I explained to the station owner that he was responsible for securing customers' cars from thieves, he admitted no liability. I threatened legal action if he didn't compensate me for the damage, and he said "Go ahead." I won a judgment for $850, which he paid on the spot. It was worth it.

When two written requests don't persuade, call and politely ask what the problem is. People don't usually ignore requests just to annoy you. Something is keeping them from complying. Try to find out what that is and work with them to overcome

### Sample Second Request, Including Threat

**To:** All Managers and Administrative Personnel
**From:** Jim Devon, Manager, Mailroom & Shipping Services
**Re:** <u>Second Request</u>: Please Use Cost-Center Codes on Outgoing Mail

As a follow-up to my earlier memo, I repeat: *Please be sure that your <u>cost-center code</u> is on all outgoing mail*. While almost all outgoing mail now comes to us with cost-center codes, there are still exceptions.

<u>Please note</u>: As of the first of next month, any outgoing mail that comes to the mailroom without a cost-center code <u>will be returned to senders</u> so they can put the cost-center code on it. I have spoken with Mike DiPippio, Vice President, Operations, and he has approved this course of action.

Again, if you do not know your cost-center code, you can get it by calling me (ext. 653) or Ann Baxter (ext. 311) in Accounting. Thank you for your cooperation in this small but important cost-control measure.

it, or if necessary, adjust your time frame while they sort things out.


## Persuasive Proposals

In most lines of business, a written proposal follows an accepted form and format. A sales proposal discusses the product or service and the requirements, function, benefits, price, and delivery. A book proposal describes the content, authors, and competitive books, and includes the table of contents and a sample chapter. A business plan or investment proposal describes the business's management, operations, finances, and need for funds.

A proposal is a sales document, but it should be free of hype and focus on solid content, unlike, say, a marketing piece. Yet a proposal need not be exhaustive to be persuasive. You need to do comprehensive research and planning, but you don't need to include it all. Give readers the information they need to understand the business opportunity and how you will exploit it, rather than bury them in data. If you have a lot of data, include them as an appendix or in a separate document.

## OUTLINE FOR A PROPOSAL

### Introduction
o *Summarize your understanding of the persuadee's needs.*

o *Describe what you're offering to meet those needs.*

### Deliverables
o *Provide the details of whatever you are selling, offering, or proposing.*

o *Describe the tasks you will perform.*

o *Mention any warranties or guarantees in this section.*

### Time Frame

○ *Specify the delivery date or deadline for completing the tasks.*

### Responsibilities

○ *Describe what each party would be responsible for doing, providing, or paying.*

○ *Include details such as delivery, installation, training, follow-up, and so on.*

### Compensation

○ *State any amounts that will be paid or invested.*

○ *Mention terms and schedule of payments.*

### Conclusion

○ *Note that you are sure the persuadee will be satisfied.*

○ *Thank the persuadee for his or her consideration.*

Space does not permit me to provide a sample proposal here, and there are too many different types of proposals. However, a number of Web sites and books provide guidance on writing proposals. Go to your favorite search engine or online bookstore and enter keywords such as "writing sales proposals," "writing business plans," or "writing grant proposals," and you will find guidance on the subject.

## Letters of Complaint

Even after an outfit you do business with screws up, you may have to persuade them to put things right. Use the telephone first, but if that doesn't work, writing often will. Writing helps you present the problem clearly, without expressing emotions that will work against you.

Writing is also the best way to get a senior executive's attention. That executive will pass the complaint to someone else, but it will get priority because it came from that executive.

**Take Action**

*See the book* How to Complain *by attorney Mel Stein for tips on dealing with companies that have wronged you.*

## *OUTLINE FOR A LETTER OF COMPLAINT:*

**Paragraph #1**

○ *Cite your relationship with the company—for instance, how long you've done business with them, who recommended you, or the reason you chose them.*

○ *Introduce your problem.*

**Paragraph #2**

○ *Explain the problem.*

○ *Cite the steps, if any, that have been taken to resolve the problem.*

○ *Document continuing instances of the problem and failure to solve it, or why you feel the proposed solution is*

unfair or inadequate, which may take
a separate paragraph.

### Paragraph #3

○ Tell the company your solution and
when you want it implemented.

○ If it will help your case, and you have
acceptable alternatives, mention them.

### Closing Paragraph

○ Close as pleasantly and positively as
you can.

○ Mention a specific follow-up step that
you will take, and a date.

## Sample Complaint Letter

Dear Mr. Contractor,

As we've discussed in several phone conversations over the past two weeks, we have
a serious unresolved problem with our kitchen renovation project. This is particularly dis-
appointing because you came highly recommended by the Custom Cabinet Cooperative.

Because your employees did not follow the specifications provided in the plans
from our architect, there is too little room for the models of stove and dishwasher we
specified. Against my specific instructions, your foreman ordered your crew to install
cabinetry before delivery of the appliances, assuring me, "It'll be okay."

Now that the appliances have arrived, it's not okay. They do not fit, and your foreman wants to cut the cabinetry in order to make them fit. This is not an acceptable
solution, and I have forbidden him to cut the cabinets or to order them to be cut. I know
you are busy, but my family must have full use of our kitchen by Thanksgiving, or your
company will be in breach of contract.

Please contact me immediately so that we can discuss ways to resolve this serious
problem. You may reach me at the office (999-999-9000) or on my cell (999-999-7777).

Sincerely,

**Bob Field**

## Collection Letters: Get the Money

If you work in or own a company that sells merchandise on credit, your credit manager or accountant will have a series of standard collection letters. These letters are usually sent after an account is thirty days past due, then every thirty days until you are paid. Each letter in the series expresses increasingly greater urgency and consequences.

I won't reproduce collection letters here because they are readily available elsewhere, and because they are standard. Such letters are used by banks and other lenders to businesses and consumers, as well as by businesses that sell on credit.

To be persuasive, collection letters should mention the amount, remind the recipient of the benefits of a good bill-paying record, and use words such as "unpleasant" and "unfortunate." Don't imply moral judgment in your letters, say "deadbeat" or "fraud," or make threats until you are ready to carry them out or write off the account.

> ### cred•it
>
> 1. Arrangement in which a buyer pays for goods or services after taking delivery
> 2. Money borrowed for payment at a later date, in installments or as a lump sum

## Sales Letter: Problem + Solution = $

I believe the best sales letters—and certainly the most straightforward ones—

basically present or dramatize a problem that the reader is likely to have, and then present the product or service as the solution. Effective letters also ask for the order, or at least ask the recipient to take an action that will move him or her closer to ordering.

## *OUTLINE FOR A ONE-PAGE SALES LETTER:*

### Paragraph #1

- *Dramatize a problem that the reader can relate to.*

- *Use simple language that the reader readily understands.*

### Paragraph #2

- *Tell the reader that you have the solution to this problem.*

- *Explain how your product or service solves the problem. (This may take two or three paragraphs.)*

- *If possible, show that you understand why this problem is important or difficult to solve.*

### Paragraph #3

- *Ask the reader to place an order or to request more information.*

- *Tell the reader that you will be in touch, if you intend to follow up with a phone call or e-mail.*

***Take Action***
*For information on collection letters and sample letters visit* www.creditguru .com/collection.htm

## Sample sales letter for a business product

A recent study by the American Photocopying Institute showed that <u>photocopying costs have risen 12%</u> in each of the past two years. The study showed that the increase is not due to the cost of copiers. Rather, it is the skyrocketing cost of supplies, particularly paper and toner.

I am writing to you because I can help you cut these costs sharply. In fact, if you own your own copiers or lease at favorable terms, Standard Products Inc. can <u>guarantee</u> that your cost per copy will actually <u>decrease</u> over the next year.

Standard Products can give you this guarantee because we buy in huge volume from various manufacturers and thus win deep discounts. Also, our state-of-the-art distribution network minimizes warehousing and shipping costs. We pass these savings on to you by beating whatever price you're now paying.

Of course, low prices mean nothing without high quality, so we also guarantee the quality of our paper, toner, and other supplies. The copies you get with our supplies will be as good as—or better than—your current copies. *Guaranteed*!

**To get these savings, pick up the phone and call us at 1-800-555-0300.** Tell us your current volume of usage and what you're now paying for paper and toner, and we'll fax you a proposal the next business day. (To guarantee lower prices, we do require documentation of your current prices, so be ready to mail or fax us a recent invoice.)

Don't let another year of high costs rob your profits. **Call us at 1-800-555-0300 today.**

Yours truly,

*Leon Ledbetter*

President

P.S. If you place an order with us by the 15th of this month, we will take an <u>additional</u> 10% off the price of that first order. Call now and start saving!

Notice the use of elements of format such as bold type, underscoring, and italics. Don't overuse them, but they are a must in sales letters, which people often only glance at before discarding.

## THREE STEPS TO BETTER WRITING

- *Learn basic grammar and punctuation*

- *Use three separate steps: plan, draft, edit*

- *Proofread, then read it aloud*

Also, always make a compelling case for your product or service, and ask for action. The next chapter provides more information on persuasive selling.

" EVERY SALE HAS **FIVE BASIC OBSTACLES**: NO NEED, NO MONEY, NO HURRY, NO DESIRE, NO TRUST. "

—Zig Ziglar

# Selling: Persuading Prospects to Become Customers

## 10

Selling is one of the toughest jobs in business. The entire company depends on the ability of its salespeople to bring in paying customers. That's a lot of responsibility. Also, unlike some jobs, it's very clear whether or not a salesperson is succeeding. The results are there (or not) at the end of every week, month, quarter, and year.

Those things—the importance of success and the clarity of its measures—would make the job of selling tough enough, but then you have serious barriers to success. People must be persuaded that they want, need, and should pay you for something.

**hard sell**

1. Using fast talk and pressure tactics to push people to buy
2. Method that fails to build lasting customer relationships

This chapter views selling as persuasion, but I don't see sales as talking people into buying things. That's the hard sell and the classic image of sales, and it can work. But there are methods that rely less on pushing and more on leading prospects to buy. This chapter explains those methods.

## What Do I Mean by Selling?

By selling, I mean selling on the phone or in person. Direct mail and Internet sales are forms of selling, and people sell Microsoft Word, movie tickets, and Budweiser, but demand for those things is such that the seller is an order taker. Once marketing and advertising have done their work, there's no sales resistance to overcome. This chapter focuses on selling against direct resistance.

Only companies that face sales resistance need skilled salespeople. These outfits usually sell products that are new, complicated, high priced, or all three. A lot of face-to-face (or personal) selling occurs in business-to-business (or B-to-B) sales, in which one company sells a product or service to another company. But personal selling also occurs in consumer sales, particularly in retail, automotive, and financial services businesses.

### or•der ta•kers

1. Salespeople for a usually low-priced, high-demand product
2. Delivery people for companies that use advertising, rather than selling, to move their products

Salespeople lead people to change. To see how salespeople effect change, let's review the five-stage change process presented in Chapter 2, in which people are:

- Unaware that they need to change

- Acknowledge that they probably should change

- Understand the nature of the change and their alternatives

- Commit to making the change and then take action

- Stick with the change

**Take Action**
*Check out Hugh Macfarlane's book* The Leaky Funnel *for good information on what he calls the buyer's journey.*

The salesperson makes the prospect aware of the product and then helps him acknowledge that he needs it. The salesperson presents the product's benefits and its advantages over the alternatives (including doing nothing) and helps the prospect commit to buy. After the sale, a good salesperson ensures that the customer remains happy with the purchase decision. All salespeople should understand the changes their customers go through in their journey from being unaware to buying the product.

## Prospecting: Panning for Gold

Good selling begins with good prospecting. Prospecting locates people to sell to, which means identifying potential prospects and then qualifying them as potential customers. This research is integral to successful selling.

Companies generate potential prospects, or leads, through advertising, direct mail, referrals, and telephone inquiries. Most salespeople also find their own leads. Of course, some leads are better than others. Salespeople usually use telephone leads to qualify the prospect, which involves two basic questions:

> ○ Does the person or company have a real interest in or need for the product?
>
> ○ Does the person have the money, and in B-to-B sales, the authority, to buy the product?

This is a judgment call. For instance, level-one general resistance may prompt the persuadee to say they're not interested when they might become interested *if* the right salesperson with the right product came along. So the salesperson has to get past that initial resistance and try to interest the persuadee. Similarly, a persuadee

**PROBLEMS IN PROSPECTING**

- ○ Poor qualification criteria

- ○ Ineffective lead generation

- ○ Poor prospecting skills

- ○ Fear of rejection

might lack the need, interest, or money right now, but not next week, next month, or next year.

## Finding and Qualifying Prospects

In most businesses, finding good prospects depends on:

- *Having useful, clear qualification criteria*

- *Presenting your product or service clearly and attractively (and, often, repeatedly)*

- *Engaging the prospect and asking qualification questions*

- *Making prospecting part of your regular weekly schedule*

I can't overemphasize the need to pursue the right sales prospects, especially if you can't afford advertising or public relations to generate awareness. The best prospects genuinely need your product; have the money to pay you and the power to make the purchase; and allow you to sell with a reasonable amount of time, effort, and cost.

You can even rate prospects, say on a scale of one to five, on each of these three dimensions. For instance:

***Take Action***
*See* Sales and Marketing the Six Sigma Way *by Michael J. Webb and Tom Gorman (yes, that's me) for solid information on finding and qualifying prospects.*

**Need for what you sell:**

1     2     3     4     5

**Can pay for and approve the purchase:**

1     2     3     4     5

**Require reasonable sales efforts and costs:**

1     2     3     4     5

You can apply these criteria to potential prospects to compile lists of leads based on information from the Web; from association directories; and from newspapers, magazines, and other media, and then total and compare their ratings to decide which prospects to pursue.

### Presenting Your Product

Leaving aside advertising, public relations, and face-to-face meetings, the main ways of presenting your product or service to prospects are by mail, phone, or Web site. Unless you sell your product by direct mail, the best use of mail for most businesses is to introduce yourself with the goal of improving your chances of getting prospects on the phone (by using a letter like the sample in Chapter 9).

When you get a prospect on the phone, tell them quickly what you're selling and then ask a question. That way you avoid a canned pitch and engage the persuadee right away.

## Engaging—and Qualifying—the Prospect

Once you have a potential prospect on the phone, deliver an opening along these lines:

**Office supplies:** Hello, I'm Diane Gold, an independent sales rep for several office-supplies manufacturers. Being an independent rep allows me to get you the best price on paper, toner cartridges, and other basics, and I'd like to work up a proposal for you. Can you give me an idea of how much paper and toner you use?

**Marketing:** Hello, I'm Mike Montgomery, a specialist in marketing communications that boost sales for consulting firms. I'd like to learn a bit about your needs in that area. Can you tell me about the kind of communications you currently put out to potential customers?

Note that Diane talks about saving money, and Mike talks about making it. Very often the prospect will want to know more about you before divulging information, and that's fine. Tell them whatever they want to know about you. The goal is to start a conversation.

## Setting Up Meetings

There are several formulas for setting up meetings, some of which involve an assumptive close. The assumptive close gives the prospect two choices, either of which you'd be happy with, for instance, "Would you like that vacuum cleaner in red or blue?" For setting up appointments, it goes like this: "I'd like to meet with you, and I'm going to be in your area next Wednesday. Would the morning or afternoon work better for you?"

## Science Fuels Innovation

Scientific research in areas such as ceramics, plastics, adhesives, and lasers find their way into the market through what's known as applied science (applications), and products (innovations). Applications of ceramics would be in kitchen appliances and dental implants; applications of lasers would speed measurement and sound production. These result in products from companies such as Hotpoint (appliances), Lifecore (implants), Escort Radar Detectors, and Sony.

Of course, if the prospect doesn't want a meeting, asking in this way won't get you one. So, I usually say, "Given what you've told me, I believe it might be worthwhile for us to meet in person. Do you agree?"

If they don't agree, I don't want to meet them. If they do agree, then finding a time is usually easy.

## What About Pushing?

It may seem as if I'm presenting a rosy view of selling here, one in which you lead the prospect forward like The Sales Whisperer. You may think I believe that customers never need a push. Well, I don't, and they do. But the way you go about it is key.

Remember trust? Unless the customer trusts you, when you push they'll push back. Customers know your goal is to make a sale. So when you ask for a meeting, an order, or a check, they know what's going on.

If you've done your job up to whatever point you've reached, the prospect is probably okay with being gently pushed. It's your role to get the customer to commit, not the customer's role to get you to commit. So all along the way make sure that you tie down the steps in the sale, that is, the steps in their change process.

Be sure you address the concerns of anyone who will be affected by the product or service, and anyone who can nix the transaction. Make sure that all requirements for the product or service to work well—space, training, delivery and so on—are in place. Make sure that all financial aspects, such as the payment schedule,

**Take Action**
*To learn what you can about selling by reading, see* How to Master the Art of Selling *by Tom Hopkins and The New Strategic Selling by Robert B. Miller.*

credit approvals, or loan arrangements have been discussed and finalized. The last thing you want is a last-minute glitch.

## Have Various Lead-ins and Levels

If you work for a good-sized company, it has its product line and will experiment with new offerings and various levels of pricing and service. If you work for yourself or for a small company, you have to do that yourself.

### Starting Small with Customers

A marketing consultant I know offers to audit prospects' communications among customers, employees, investors, suppliers, lenders, and so on. He charges $1,200 to $2,400 for this service, well below his fee for a full-blown project. Many financial planners and accountants offer free diagnostics, which let them learn about the prospect's needs while letting the prospect learn about them. This builds trust while demonstrating the service provider's expertise.

In my line of work—ghostwriting books—I found I do better by offering more than just books. It costs a lot of money to get a book done, and not all potential clients are willing to make a major commitment. So I offer to write articles, white papers, sales letters, and Web site copy.

Although it's not my preferred way of working with clients, these entry-level services often lead to book projects.

It's good to have low-priced or even free offerings in your sales process. Remember, much of the resistance you encounter comes from asking people to take steps they aren't ready to take. So if you sell a big-ticket product or service, smaller-step offerings can pave the way to the larger sale.

## The Three Basic Persuaders

Once you have engaged the prospect, established rapport, and gauged his needs, you have three issues to deal with in the persuasion process: your value, differentiators, and price. These issues address the prospect's three major points of resistance, usually expressed in some form of the following questions:

Q: **Why do I need your product or service?**
A: *The value you'll derive from it.*

Q: **Why should I buy yours instead of someone else's?**
A: *Because ours will better meet your needs.*

Q: **What will it cost me?**
A: *A fair price, given the value you'll derive from it.*

Selling always deals with these three questions in some form, and you must answer them—unless you honestly cannot. In other words, if the customer won't derive value from your product, or another product would serve him better, or the price doesn't correspond to the value he'll receive, you should move on to the next prospect (or perhaps to a new employer).

## Emphasize Value as the Difference

The great tradeoff with any product service is quality versus price. Although the conversation occurs in various ways, the basic exchange is this:

> **Seller:** "I can give you great quality at a high price *or* moderate quality at a moderate price *or* low quality at a low price."
>
> **Buyer:** "I'll take high quality at a low price!"

Of course the buyer wants the impossible, but we all want high quality at a low price—just like we all want a seven-day weekend and hangover-free rum drinks. Companies try to deliver the highest possible quality for a given price, but some do it better than others, and a company's quality-price advantage can now be quickly duplicated, because the information and technology for doing so are available.

This makes the role of the salesperson incredibly important for many products. For instance, if all networking software or all telecom services or all copiers have pretty much the same price-quality (or price-performance) ratio, then the salesperson's skill at helping the buyer by providing information, assessing his needs, understanding his problems, and tailoring solutions becomes a major differentiator. The salespeople—and his relationships with customers—can become more important than the product or service itself.

## Focus on What Matters to the Customer

As a salesperson you can't just say, "Buy from me because I'm your salesperson!" You must demonstrate your value to the prospect. You must also alert the prospect to any differences that exist between your product or service and those of competitors as long as the customer cares about them.

Too many salespeople focus on differentiators the customer doesn't care about. They'll talk about all the wonderful colors the product comes in, without ascertaining which color the customer wants. They'll tout the colossal power of the unit, without first learning how much power the customer needs. They'll emphasize the product's many features, without learning which ones the customer wants.

## What's Wrong about This?

When I meet a salesperson who questions me skillfully, I am flabbergasted. What sort of lawn mower are you thinking about, electric or gas? What have you been using? How large is your yard? Does it have hills? How often do you mow? Who else might use the mower? Instead it's usually, "We have this one for $169, and that one for $249," and I have to question the salesperson about them.

Many people hold the same mistaken belief about selling as they do about persuasion in general—that it's about talking instead of listening. If persuasion is more about the persuadee than the persuader, that goes triple for selling.

## Justify Your Price

There are three basic pricing strategies: cost-plus pricing, competitive pricing, and value pricing. Each can be defined as follows:

- In cost-plus pricing, the company takes the total cost of making and selling the product and sets the price to achieve a certain level of profit.

- In competitive pricing, the company tries to beat the competition by pricing its product lower but delivering the same or better quality as competitors.

- In value pricing, the company delivers very high quality or performance and prices the product accordingly.

The customer isn't concerned with your pricing problems; he's concerned about the price he has to pay, and what he gets for his money. Customers know they can't really get high quality at a low price, so they try to get the level of quality they need for the best price they can. Your job as salesperson is to show them that that's what you deliver.

## How to Deal with Comparison Shoppers

Sometimes customers will take your price, shop around, come back to you, and ask you to meet or beat the price they got from a competitor. (At this point, you may become the persuadee!) The first thing to do in any comparison-shopping situation is to learn the details of the offer. There are usually differences in quality, performance, durability, service, maintenance requirements, or in the seller's dependability, reputation, or experience.

Then point out the differences between your product, service, or offer and the competing one. If the price difference is large, as soon as you hear it say, "I know this business inside out, and I know that it's impossible to deliver what I'm offering you at the price you've been quoted. So let's walk through this and see if we're comparing apples and apples."

Then list and compare all the features, while citing the features the customer cares about most. Point out the differences and use logical arguments to show the customer that, on a point-by-point comparison, your offer is superior even at the higher price. This will usually come down to better quality, performance, durability, or service. Finally, you can:

○ Discuss your value and the fairness of your price; in other words, explain why your price is what it is. There are usually good reasons for things being more expensive.

- Depending on your reading of the customer, either lower your price a little or politely refuse to back off, so he knows he's getting a good deal. Either way, he's reassured.

- Throw in something extra, such as training, a service contract, or an enhanced warranty to show that you mean business.

Customers who bargain with you typically have emotional as well as logical motives. They want to feel that they got a good deal—or won a victory. They want to brag to colleagues or friends (or their boss) that they bargained hard. They want assurances that you really want their business and will fight for it, or that your price really is firm and therefore the right price. It's all part of the game.

## Seal the Deal

When someone is persuaded—that is, when they've logically decided that they want or need your product, and that they trust you and can accept your price—obtaining final agreement is usually straightforward. But not always. So ask them to take the final step, and to agree to a specific time frame. Especially in a complex sale, don't accept vague assurances that things are going to "move forward

## Sample Script Securing Financial Agreement

**Persuadee:** We'll start working on this in the next week or so.

**Persuader:** Great, let's firm up the details. We'll need a letter of agreement. I'll prepare one and have it to you by the 10th. What's the process for getting an agreement like this approved?

**Persuadee:** Well, for this size fee, our finance VP has to sign off, and so would an operations manager. I'm VP of operations, so that's no problem.

**Persuader:** What about the VP of finance?

**Persuadee:** Marie's in our Brussels office until the end of next month.

**Persuader:** So should I send her a copy, or can you fax it or overnight it to her?

**Persuadee:** I'll sign it as soon as I get it, as long as it covers everything we talked about. Then I'll fax it to Marie and she can fax it back, and we're set to go.

**Persuader:** Okay. You'll sign it and fax it to Brussels. When will we get it back?

**Persuadee:** Within forty-eight hours.

**Persuader:** Great. I'll be ready to start the project on the 20th.

over the next few weeks." Instead, clearly identify the next steps and when you, and they, will take them.

If the customer is not convinced and comfortable, your setting things in motion or requesting a tangible commitment may prompt them to back out. This is not necessarily a bad thing. You can deal with a refusal by thanking them for their time, moving on to the next prospect, and leaving the door open for them to change their minds, if that would benefit you.

At least you know where you stand with a refusal. In my experience, it's often worse to deal with people who can't say no than it is to deal with those who can. It's a huge problem in sales, where basically the deal goes down to "no decision."

## THE HISTORY OF SELLING

o *Pushing product*

o *Touting features*

o *Selling benefits*

o *Creating value for customers*

**REAL SUCCESS** IS FINDING YOUR LIFEWORK IN THE WORK THAT YOU LOVE.

"

—David McCullough

# Find Work in Any Market

## 11

Searching for a job can be dark and lonely work. The stakes are high, the balance of power seems tilted toward the hiring authority, and the rejection seems quite personal. Of course, if you are in a profession or hold a skill that's in high demand, these factors are mitigated, and you may even find them trying to persuade you.

But this chapter focuses on situations where you, as job seeker, must persuade someone to hire you. The job search isn't always about persuasion but the interviews usually are, and it's in your interest to negotiate the best salary and benefits package that you can. So let's look at persuasive interviewing and salary negotiation.

## Getting Interviews

In discussing targeting persuadees in Chapter 4, I mentioned the shotgun and rifle-shot approaches, which describe the two main ways of getting interviews.

In a shotgun job search, you approach a large number of broadly targeted companies in a standard way, usually with the

## THE EMPLOYMENT PICTURE

- *Little mutual loyalty*

- *Permanent job insecurity*

- *Rapid, unexpected change*

- *More opportunities for off-staff workers*

**Take Action**

*Be sure that you not only read but also do the exercises in Richard Nelson Bolles's* What Color Is Your Parachute? *It's the best job-search guide I've ever read.*

same cover letter and resume. You don't research the companies in much depth. Instead you play the percentages, reasoning that your education and experience will entice someone to interview you.

In a rifle-shot job search, you approach a few carefully targeted companies in a more customized manner. You gather information on ten to twenty companies, and then create a short list of those you'd truly like to join. You research them, approach the person who heads the area that interests you, and interview them for information—a technique popularized, if not invented, by Richard Nelson Bolles.

I prefer the rifle-shot approach because it gives you knowledge, which is power. When you know a company's history, structure, management, and strategy, you see how you might fit in and be of service. When you finally approach the company, you do so with confidence that's very hard to fake.

## People Hire People

No matter how imposing the organizing, how difficult the position, or how bad the job market, it is people who hire people. If people do the hiring, those people can be persuaded to hire you. In this light, thinking of the hiring process as a process of persuasion may be the best possible mindset because in the hiring process you must:

- Break through initial resistance to get an interview

- Use rational arguments to neutralize specific resistance and convince the hiring authority that you can do the job

- Use emotional appeals to show the person doing the hiring that you want the job and will do it well—and will fit into the organization—and thus overcome ultimate resistance.

### hir·ing auth·or·i·ty

1. Person who makes the final decision on hiring for a specific position
2. Usually the manager to whom the position will report

### hir·ing pro·cess

1. Procedures for a new hire, including interviewing, checking references, and extending the job offer
2. Hurdles that the job seeker must clear in order to be hired

## Dealing with Job Interviews

If you need a job, your goal in job interviews is to get a job offer. I've seen candidates who don't seem to realize this. They focus on learning about the company, on the give and take of the interview process, and so on. That's all fine, but I'm talking about persuasion.

The get-an-offer mindset helps you focus. It helps you avoid saying things that move you away from an offer, and guides you to say things that move you toward one. For example, if you need a full-time job, don't bring up your dream of hitting the road with your band to support your self-produced alt-rock CD.

To get an offer you must persuade the interviewers—and there will usually be more than one—that you can do the job, want to do the job, and fit the organizational culture. If you fail to persuade them of any of these three points, you won't get an offer. This means convincing them of your competence, desire, and likability.

### Competence: I Can Do It

Most of the questions in any job interview are geared to gauging your competence because it's the easiest of the three factors to judge and measure. Most interviewers gauge your ability to do a job based on your experience in doing the job, or one very much like it. For entry-level positions, they look more to grades, extracurricular activities, part-time work, and internships.

They are looking for evidence that you have the skills, or at least the aptitude, for the job. The key, then, is to give them examples of your past successes in the job or in situations where you used the skills. For instance, don't say, "I'm a people person," or "I've always liked working with numbers" without providing an example of how well you work with people or numbers.

They're also looking for communication and problem-solving skills. You demonstrate the former in the interviews and in anything you give them in writing, so be sure your cover letter, resume, and writing samples are well written and error free. You demonstrate the latter in your responses to questions like those you'll learn about in the behavioral interview mentioned later in this chapter.

*Take Action*
*See the* Knock 'em Dead *series by Martin Yate for great job-search ideas.*

## Desire: I Want to Do It

Here's where research on the company pays off handsomely. Nothing shows genuine interest in a company more than your efforts to learn about the place. Don't show off, but make it clear that you know the company and its history and industry.

Things you should know when you interview for a professional or managerial position include:

- *The name and tenure of the chief executive officer and chief operating officer*

- *News stories about the organization over the past year or two, and major events in its history, such as a merger or a breakthrough product*

- *Key markets, customers, products and services*

- *Major competitors and recent industry developments*

○ Stated mission, and the company's
strategy to achieve it

These things are easy to learn, especially via the Internet. Speaking of which,
you are looking for solid information and
the official story, not dirt, scuttlebutt, or
nonsense. For instance, don't bring up
consumer lawsuits or the company's ties
to lobbyists to show that you are in the
know. However, at the company's Web
site, check out speeches, remarks at con-
ferences, and quotes from press releases
or from the CEO to get a fix on the organization's strategy.

If—no, make that when—an interviewer asks you, "Why would you like to
come to work for us?" say specific things
that show sincere interest and a willingness to contribute to the mission. Without research you might either parrot back
what the interviewer has said or mouth
platitudes instead of convincing the hiring
authority of your sincerity.

## Likableness: You're
## Comfortable with Me
People like being with people who are
fun to be with, particularly in industries such as advertising and entertain-
ment, but the main thing is that they feel
comfortable with you. People feel comfort-

able with positive, easygoing people who display a good energy level.

By a good energy level I mean a medium level. High energy appeals to some people and for some positions, but can come off as hyperactivity to others; low energy may signify that you're laid back, but can seem like depression or lethargy to some interviewers.

Project competence and seriousness, but also with a bit of humor. The humor should be situational, rather than jokes, and light. Avoid black humor unless you know you've got the right audience. Also avoid self-deprecating humor, cracks about your OCD, or references to mind-altering substances or your failed love life. In fact, say nothing negative about yourself. Demonstrate that you like yourself, even if you don't.

## Be Honest, But . . .

As a headhunter I met a candidate who felt he had to tell interviewers he was a recovering alcoholic. I advised him not to, but he said he could work only for people who knew this. I saw his point and knew that some interviewers would too. But I felt others might perceive instability, feel uncomfortable, or worry about him backsliding. Better to mention this after landing the job, unless you're applying to Seagram's.

## Arguments and Appeals

The key rational arguments for the decision to hire you are:

- *You have the skills and education to do the job.*

- *You have the experience to do the job because you've either succeeded in it in the past, or you've succeeded in jobs requiring similar skills.*

- *You will succeed in the job because you have succeeded in past endeavors.*

- *You are genuinely interested in joining the company, as evidenced by the research you've done and the questions you ask.*

## The main emotional appeals are:

- *You admire the company and its style—the corporate culture it projects—and you mention that.*

- *You like the people you've met during the interviews and you've thanked them for considering you, verbally and in a follow-up note or e-mail.*

- *You have put people at ease by being friendly and interested in them.*

- *You want the job and you told them you are excited by the possibility of joining the company.*

# Types of Job Interviews

Broadly there are four types of job interviews: the behavioral interview, the panel interview, the conversational interview, and the stress interview. Some interviewers combine two or more of these types. And then there's the luncheon interview.

Here's how each one works.

## Behavioral Interview

In the behavioral interview, the interviewer asks questions to find evidence for certain behaviors and personality characteristics. The questions are often along the lines of "Give me an example of a time when you performed under pressure," or "I'm a customer, you're a service rep, and I've accused you of overcharging me. What do you say?"

Your answer should demonstrate how you respond to pressure or interact with people. So don't just say, "I usually handle pressure well," or "I'd say that we couldn't have overcharged him." Instead, describe how you would deal with or have dealt with these situations. You might describe a problem-solving approach you use—such as Gather Information, Analyze the Situation, and Decide—and give an example of how you've used it. *Show* them you have the skills and personality for the job.

## TYPES OF INTERVIEWS

- Behavioral
- Conversational
- Panel
- Stress
- Luncheon

### Conversational Interview

A conversational interview is an interview conducted as a conversation, and it's the most common type. Some conversational interviewers are unprepared or hire mainly on chemistry, but most of them have "pet" questions. Don't think it's just a conversation, because you are definitely being judged. Stay focused, and, whenever possible, answer questions with specific examples.

### Panel Interview

In the panel interview, you face two or more interviewers at the same time, who usually use a combination of the behavioral and conversational styles. At the outset, write down the interviewers' names and titles. Maintain eye contact mainly with the person who asked you the question, but glance at the others as your reply.

### Stress Interview

Ah, the dreaded stress interview. In this one the interviewer may seem irritable, fire off one question after another, or challenge you somehow. Remain calm and don't take it personally. You are being tested for how you deal with pressure and unpredictability.

Answer the questions as you would in any interview, citing examples and displaying good manners. If the interviewer rushes you, repeat the question back to him to buy some time to develop your answer. Fortunately, the stress interview is relatively rare, but you may run across it.

## The Luncheon Interview

If you are interviewed over lunch, you've got a bit more to deal with. In fact, stress interviews over lunch often degenerate into food fights (just kidding). Interviews over lunch are almost always conversational and you are supposed to relax and reveal who you are.

### Testing for Testiness

Many organizations gauge candidates' personalities with psychological tests. My advice is don't try to game these tests. You might come out looking like you've got the very personality disorder you think you're masking. Besides, if they don't want someone with your personality, do you want to work there? I was hired by two major companies that used these tests, and I wasn't cut out for corporate life.

Of course, that's the problem. There's a behavioral element to a lunch interview. If your waiter scalds you with coffee and you go into a spirited pain dance and hold forth on his status at birth, you won't look good. Here are some hints for surviving the luncheon interview:

○ *Arrive early, check your coat, check your appearance in the restroom mirror, and wait in the bar or hostess area.*

○ *Order a dish you can eat with minimal mess and effort; this is not the time for baby back ribs. Have club soda or ice tea rather than alcohol or cola.*

○ *Relax, but mind your manners and treat the waiter or waitress with courtesy.*

○ *Follow the interviewer's lead and find personal things that you have in common.*

○ *Thank them for lunch when they pay for it, and when you part tell them you enjoyed it.*

Actually, it's hard for all but the most seasoned job seekers to enjoy a lunch interview. After all, it is work just like any other interview—hardly a festive occasion.

## Persuading Them

Most positions are designed so that any reasonably intelligent, educated, well-adjusted individual can perform them. So how can you distinguish yourself? By showing not only that you can do the job, but also that you want it more than anyone else the company has interviewed. Here are five ways to convince them:

- *Ask on-point questions about the company's direction and strategy, and how the parts—including your prospective job—fit together.*

- *Tell them that you've always respected the company, and tell them why; always be specific and cite examples whenever you say something good about the place, or it will sound like hooey.*

- *Mention that you've liked the people you've met in your interviews, and could see yourself joining them as part of the team.*

- *Tell them you want the job; at some point late in the interview say something like, "I want to tell you flat out, although I know you have your process to go through at your end, I am extremely interested in joining your organization and believe that I could make a real contribution." Be prepared to explain that contribution with specifics.*

- *Get a sense of the company's time frame for moving to the next step; if you don't hear from them in that time, call the hiring manager and ask how the process is going.*

In my experience too many people go through job interviews displaying a vague sense that someone should be courting them. Always remember, unless you are a proven moneymaker or are in high demand, *you* are courting *them*.

## How to Handle a Job Offer

It's the employer's place to make the compensation offer, but interviewers may ask about your salary expectations. If they do, be vague but positive. "The important thing is the position and the contribution I could make. If those are right, I'm sure we can agree on compensation." If they ask again, say, "I'd like to reserve that information at this point."

> The world is full of willing people, some willing to work, the rest willing to let them.
> —**Robert Frost**

Generally, the offer it will come from the hiring manager, that is, your prospective boss, or a human resources manager. With few exceptions I'd say *never* accept an offer on the spot. Say you will need a couple of days, or until Friday or Monday, to consider it. Why?

Because the compensation package for most professional and managerial jobs is too complex for you to deal with on the spot. Depending on the job, you might have to consider:

- *Base salary, signing bonus, and annual bonus*

- *Profit sharing, or stock or stock options*

- *Retirement benefits, such as a 401(k) or pension plan*

- *Paid or partially paid health, dental, disability, and life insurance*

- *Paid vacation and personal days, and flextime or telecommuting opportunities*

- *Items such as tuition reimbursement, relocation assistance, company car, and financial planning assistance*

Many companies, particularly major corporations, still offer complete benefits. Small companies often offer profit sharing or stock potentially worth tens of thousands of dollars—or more—if the company grows. When you are young, health care and disability insurance may seem irrelevant, but a major accident or illness makes them incredibly important. So consider what is most important to you, and negotiate the best compensation package that you can.

## How to Negotiate Compensation

With preparation you can usually improve the original offer. Large companies have policies and pay grades, but for the right candidate the hiring manager—or his boss—can make an exception or get a higher grade assigned to the job. This is truest for senior positions and jobs demanding special skills. Outfits such as small ad agencies and **professional services firms** have even more flexibility.

In general, a company's first offer will rarely be its best offer. They almost always leave room to increase the initial salary offer because they know most candidates will try to negotiate upward. Similarly, in any conversation about salary you should ask for a bit more than you expect. It's actually difficult for either you or your prospective employer to know what you are worth. Here are guidelines for negotiating compensation:

**pro•fess•ion•al ser•vi•ces firms**

1. Traditionally, law, accounting, architecture, or engineering firms
2. Broadly, any firm providing advertising, consulting, design, technology, or similar business services

- Understand how much leverage you have, but don't overestimate or think that you must win on all points. The more unique and in demand your skills, the greater your leverage.

- Decide what's truly important to you—minimum salary, health insurance, flexibility to work at home—and focus on those things.

- Phrase things as requests and support them with reasons. In other words, if necessary, tell the company why certain things are important to you.

Maybe they can find another way to meet those needs while staying within company policies.

○ If they counter your reasons with points that you can't counter, make a note of their point and think it over. You can then call later that day or the next day, and talk it over.

○ Take notes, and when you receive your offer letter and statement of benefits, check them against your notes and address anything that's out of kilter.

Approach the negotiation with confidence. They've decided to hire you, and you need only work out the terms. Don't argue or ask for the impossible, and know that they have the most flexibility on things like salary, signing bonuses, and relocation expenses. Keep things businesslike because you are going to have to work with these folks, but you want to do it for the best compensation you can arrange.

> In business as in life, you don't get what you deserve. You get what you negotiate.
> **—Charles Karrass**